In the
BEGINNING

*The True Message of the
Genesis Origin Stories*

LAWRENCE R. FARLEY

ANCIENT FAITH PUBLISHING
CHESTERTON, INDIANA

Published by:
    Ancient Faith Publishing
    A Division of Ancient Faith Ministries
    P.O. Box 748
    Chesterton, IN 46304

ISBN: 978-1-944967-39-0

Printed in the United States of America

Library of Congress Cataloging-in-Publication Data

Names: Farley, Lawrence R., author.
Title: In the beginning : the true message of the Genesis origin stories /
    Lawrence R. Farley.
Description: Chesterton, Indiana : Ancient Faith Publishing, 2018.
Identifiers: LCCN 2018001078 | ISBN 9781944967390 (pbk.)
Subjects: LCSH: Bible. Genesis, I-XI--Criticism, interpretation, etc.
Classification: LCC BS1235.52 .F37 2018 | DDC 222/.1106--dc23
LC record available at https://lccn.loc.gov/2018001078

Contents

Dedicated to
the Very Reverend Dr. Chad Hatfield,
with deepest respect and abiding gratitude

INTRODUCTION

A New Hexameron

IN ABOUT THE YEAR 370, St. Basil the Great began preaching a sermon series in his church during Great Lent. He preached nine sermons, in both the morning and the evening services, to his congregation of humble working men. (In his third homily he spoke of the "many artisans belonging to mechanical trades crowding around" him.) He worked through the stories of the six days of creation, expounding the text verse by verse. He preached off the cuff (the work shows none of the detailed polish of his literary book *On the Holy Spirit*), and apparently he wowed them.

The sermons were written down and published as *The Hexameron* (meaning "the six days," from the Greek root words for "six"—*hexa*, and "days"—*ameron*). The book became something of a bestseller and was read and praised by Ss. Photius, Jerome, and of course Basil's friend, Gregory of Nazianzus. The last was especially complimentary: "Whenever I take his *Hexameron* in hand," he wrote, "and quote its words, I am brought face to face with my Creator; I begin to understand the method of creation; I feel more awe than ever I did before, when I only looked at God's work with my eyes." Gregory eventually produced his own version of the *Hexameron*, as did many others. Expounding on the creation stories became almost a growth industry. It became a specific genre of theological exposition, a kind of hexameral literature.

This is not surprising. Questions of origin are fundamental to our self-understanding. Even children will ask the question, "Mommy, where did I come from?" and philosophers have not ceased to echo the same question on a deeper level. Knowing where we came from is key to understanding who and what we are—and therefore how we should live and behave. We see this reflected in the lectionary of the Orthodox Church: during the services of the Presanctified Gifts in Great Lent, the Church reads from the Book of Genesis (to tell us who we are) and from the Book of Proverbs (to tell us how to live). The two are linked, not only in the lectionary, but in life.

When St. Basil first preached his homilies to his working-class flock in the late fourth century, he of course spoke as a man of his time. That meant he was limited not only by the scientific understanding of his contemporaries, but also by his literary diet. Thus he read and knew about the scientific and religious interpretations of Orthodox, pagan, and heretical writers, but not about the writers of the ancient Near East.[1] He had never read the Sumerian *Song of the Hoe*, or *Enki and Ninmah*, the Akkadian *Atrahasis*, or the *Enuma Elish*, or the Egyptian *Instruction of Merikare*—indeed, archaeology then had not yet begun to unearth such literary treasures. St. Basil and his patristic colleagues therefore read the Genesis texts through the only lenses available to them.

Fortunately, the abiding lessons of those texts lay on the surface, in the details of the stories themselves, so that we have the patristic gold even if the Fathers did not have the hermeneutical tools to delve deeper and read the stories as parts of an ancient literature. As Orthodox Christians, we inherit that gold and remain committed to the Fathers who bequeathed it to us. But gratitude and loyalty to the Fathers do not require us to refuse to use the tools now available

---

1   The excessive and arbitrary use of allegory in some heretical writers gave St. Basil an added appreciation for the literal meaning. As he says in one of his *Hexameron* sermons, "When I hear 'grass' [in the text] I think of grass, and in the same manner I understand everything as it is said."

or to disdain the insights that using those tools can bring. Indeed, the frequent patristic references to Berossus, a Babylonian priest in the third century BC, show the Fathers were happy to dig back as far as they could in their search for scriptural truth.[2] In fact, their use of Berossus invites us to use the tools available to us today, and read afresh the Genesis creation stories in the light of ancient Near Eastern literature and hermeneutics.

This fresh reading is especially needful because of the warfare being waged over the historicity of the Book of Genesis. Whether it be in the interminable debates about the validity of the theory of evolution or the search for the original Adam and Eve somewhere in Africa, we see that for many people the credibility of the Christian Faith depends upon the reliability of the creation stories. I remember one earnest young man in church preparing to leave the Faith because he could not find dinosaurs in the first chapter of Genesis.

The bare-knuckle battle between science and religion, as old as it is pointless, still rages in our culture. It is just here that another look at the first chapters of Genesis may help end the battle and free up its combatants to pursue other, more fruitful topics. It is time, I suggest, with gratitude to St. Basil, for a new *Hexameron* for a new generation. In the pages that follow, we will take a fresh look at not only the narrative of the first six days of creation, but all the origin stories in the first eleven chapters of the Book of Genesis.

Situating the Stories

It is tempting for anyone entangled in the supposed conflict between science and religion, trading blows with the evolutionists (as some call them), to miss the broader context of the first eleven chapters of the Book of Genesis and focus one's thoughts and energies entirely

---

2   John Walton, *The Lost World of Adam and Eve* (Downers Grove, IL: IVP Academic, 2015), p. 23.

upon the creation stories. Admittedly the English name for the book gives us little help in broadening our perspective: the title "Genesis" comes from the Greek word meaning "beginning, origin," and we therefore imagine that the entire book is concerned with the origins of the world and how we all got here. We therefore miss the literary fact that Genesis flows seamlessly into Exodus, which flows seamlessly into Leviticus and then Numbers and Deuteronomy. In other words, the Genesis stories form part of a larger narrative, and that narrative is primarily about the people of Israel, not about the creation of the world. The story really begins in earnest with the introduction and call of Abraham in chapter twelve, and the cosmic origin stories form the backdrop of that narrative.

This is not simply chronological trivia but key to understanding the whole narrative, including especially the first eleven chapters, which are the sole concern of this present volume. Opening the first pages of the Bible in the Book of Genesis transports us back to a time of conflict. When the people of Israel left Egypt and stood trembling at the foot of Mount Sinai, and when they finally entered the Promised Land of Canaan and found innumerable Canaanites there, they stepped into a world filled with foes. The land may have been promised by God to the descendants of Abraham, but it was no more empty then than it is now, and its inhabitants had no intention of vacating their homes just because a group of rough-and-tumble former Egyptian slaves said they should. The land would have to be taken by armed force and then defended by armed vigilance. That struggle for possession and retention is recounted at length in the Books of Joshua, Judges, and Kings.

The main fact, frighteningly clear to Israel back then, is that they were by far the underdog, the little guy. They were surrounded by powers and superpowers, each one larger, stronger, better armed, and more ferocious than they were. The story of David and Goliath was their story, except that they faced not one giant, but many. The Promised Land was located in the land bridge between Africa and Asia, and if the soil of its sacred territory was not uniformly lush, its strategic location made it the place to be. The old adage of "location, location, location" proved all too true in the history of the chosen people. God told them over and over again to "fear not" (e.g., Josh. 1:6f), because humanly speaking they had every reason to be afraid.

That is the cultural and political background to the Genesis stories, and in fact to all the Old Testament. Israel lived all of its national life on the front lines of a battlefield. What gave them the courage to stay there and not flee when faced with such over-whelming odds was the conviction that the God who created the whole world, including all those scary nations staring at them across the front lines, was their own God. Yahweh (or Elohim, to give His other name) was not simply their own tribal deity, one god among many, the god who fought for Israel against the Moabites' god, Chemosh. Theological thought in their day regarded each of the gods as jurisdictional and territorial, in that Chemosh reigned supreme in Moab, and Yahweh reigned supreme in Israel. The Law and the Prophets said otherwise, insisting boldly that Yahweh, the tribal deity of little Israel, reigned supreme throughout the whole world. That meant if He wanted to give the territory (say) of Moab to Israel, He would do it, and there was absolutely nothing that Moab's Chemosh could do about it.

This is the point and the subtext of all the stories preceding the call of Abraham. The genealogies of the first chapters, boring as they may be to us, have a polemical point to them. In these geneal-ogies the narrator traces the human race from its first father, called "Adam" (the Hebrew word for "man"), to Noah, and then from Noah to Terah and his son Abram. In so doing he subtly places Israel smack in the center of the world, making it the focus and purpose of all human history. The Book of Genesis and the entire Pentateuch focus upon Israel, but the story of Israel is prefaced by stories of universal events, and the One steering those events and guiding the history of the world is none other than Israel's God, Yahweh.

We moderns tend to read about the creation of mankind by God, the first sin and its punishment, the first murder, the Flood, and the tower of Babel, and regard all these stories as mere etiology, historical explanation of how things got to be the way they now are. That is, we regard the stories primarily as explanations of origins, as the genesis of sin, death, human expansion, and division.

But seen in their proper context, these stories are more than that. They are bold assertions that the whole state of the wide world was solely the result of interaction with the tribal deity of the Hebrews. The God of Israel was not just another one of the minor deities presiding over a single region. He made every nation and people and language. This meant that the Moabites might have worshipped Chemosh, but they were fools when they did. If they only knew the history of the world, they would have known that it was Yahweh Elohim, the God of Israel, who made them and who presided over the globe as its judge and provider, and that they therefore should worship Him alone. Chemosh, along with all the other deities of all the other mighty nations opposing Israel, never did anything for anyone.

It was this subtext and message that gave the people of Israel hope when they faced down the many mighty nations intent on their destruction. The superpowers, such as the Egyptians and the Assyrians, might boast that their gods were the mightiest of all and would give them victory over all other nations. Tiny little Israel knew that those gods were idols and vanities and nothings. The One ruling over the affairs of nations was their own God, and He had promised that they would survive. More than that, He had promised that if they stayed true to Him and worshipped Him alone, He would bestow victory upon them, even if they were vastly outnumbered. Their enemies might come upon Israel one way, but they would flee before them seven ways, if only Israel would trust in God (Deut. 28:7). Large numbers meant nothing; if God's people would cleave to Him in love and worship Him only, one hundred Israelite soldiers would chase ten thousand of their foes (Lev. 26:8).

How did they know this promise was reliable? Because their God was the One who made and judged and renewed the globe. The old story said that in the beginning it was their own Elohim who created the heavens and the earth (Gen. 1:1); it was their own Yahweh who sent the flood of destruction to judge the world's sin and to renew the earth (Gen. 6:5f). It was Yahweh who came down to confuse the tongues of all men (Gen. 11:5f)—the same Yahweh who called Abram and promised that his seed would inherit the land of Canaan (Gen. 12:1f).

In reading these texts, our own familiar theology misleads us: there *is* only one God, so who else could make the heavens and the earth? But in the days of Moses and afterward, there were many gods available for such a role, and Yahweh Elohim was just one of them. Our familiar monotheism blinds us to the lesson written plainly on the page: that the gods of the nations, such as Chemosh and Molech and a hundred other deities, were nowhere in sight when the world was made. Their temples and altars may have later filled the world, but they had nothing to do with the history of the world. Yahweh Elohim and He alone made the world and presided over it as its Judge and Renewer and Savior. By prefacing the story of Yahweh's call to Abram with stories of His creating and judging and renewing the world, the narrator of Genesis pulls the gods of

Israel's foes from their thrones and declares that Israel's eventual triumph is assured.

More than that, setting the story of Israel within this cosmic context saves that story from being read as just so much insular national self-glorification. If the Book of Genesis had lacked these first eleven chapters and opened with the call of Abraham, Israel might have thought their God was indeed just a tribal god, rather like all the other gods of the nations, only perhaps a little more muscular. Their faith would have lacked its crucial cosmic dimension. Then they might have imagined that Yahweh was simply the god who was on their side, and not also the God who was on the world's side. Without its cosmic preface, the Book of Genesis would give its Israelite readers the impression that God cared only for Israel. Even with the inclusion of those precious chapters, Israel managed to be self-absorbed and insular enough.

What if those chapters with their cosmic myths and stories of universal growth, sin, judgment, and redemption had never been written? How would Israel ever guess that God loved even the pagans of Nineveh (Jon. 4:11), that He loved the Gentiles? That He loved the sinner, the prostitute, and the prodigal? The origin stories do more than simply tell us who we are and how we got here. More importantly, they tell us who our God is—the deity not only of one little people but the Creator of all, the God who cares for all the peoples of the earth.

As well as situating the early stories of Genesis within their larger context in the Genesis narrative, we must also situate them within the culture of their time. That is, we must learn to read them with the same kind of eyes with which their original recipients read them. Israel, standing at the foot of Mount Sinai and shortly afterward, did not read them in the same way as we do in our post-Enlightenment scientific culture. That is a problem, exegetically speaking, for those stories were first of all addressed not to us, but to them. We may listen to those stories also as their spiritual heirs, but we must do so standing behind the original hearers and listening over their shoulders. Otherwise we will hear the stories amiss, reading them through foreign and misleading lenses. If we interpret the text on the basis of presuppositions that are different from those of Sinaitic Israel, we are guaranteed to misinterpret it.

It can be very difficult to transpose ourselves from the twenty-first century, travel back so many years to the foot of Mount Sinai, and read the Bible differently than we have been doing. Presuppositions are often hard to detect—which of course is why they are called "*pre*suppositions." We naturally regard our own way of interpreting the text as the only possible one and find it difficult to adopt another way of interpreting the text and of looking at reality. But we have little choice: if we would hear the Word of God as it first sounded forth to its original audience, we must somehow learn to speak this foreign language—at least while we are interpreting the sacred text.

In the absence of a time machine, the only way to do this is to read up on historical texts from the period with which we are dealing—texts such as those cited above, like the *Enuma Elish*. These give us some sense of how the ancient people read and regarded creation stories like the ones in the early chapters of the Book of Genesis. Israel was of course different in some ways from the surrounding peoples, but they nonetheless shared many of the same cultural assumptions as their neighbors. Therefore, looking at the ways their neighbors viewed creation stories gives us some hints as to how Israel would have read their own stories. Exactly how they would have read these stories will become apparent in the commentary that follows. But we may be sure that reading them with modern scientific eyes and through the lenses bequeathed by the Enlightenment is sure to give us a wrong reading.

It is easy for a modern person reading the origin stories in Genesis to misunderstand the nature of the literary material. It is precisely because the author has so skillfully blended earlier sources together to form one continuous narrative that one can read it all as if it were one single literary genre—that is, as if it were all the genre of history. The narrative as it stands, though, still contains certain clues that the author was using separate sources, for we find the phrase "these are the generations of" (Heb. *toldoth*) over and over again. Each one of these *toldoth* represents a separate source, a distinct family history. The sacred author weaves them together so brilliantly into his ongoing narrative that we can almost forget the separate sources are there; the seams (e.g., references to the *toldoth*) are almost invisible. But if we look carefully, we can observe that separate sources were used.

The story of Abraham and his descendants—that is, the story of the people of Israel that comprises the rest of the Old Testament—is an historical story. Abraham, Isaac, Jacob, Moses, Joshua, and the rest of the prophets were all real people, and the stories recounted about them are historically true—written of course according to the historical canons and standards of their day, but historical nonetheless. If we regard the entire Book of Genesis as a single literary genre, we will misread it and regard the first eleven chapters as similarly historical.

Such a misreading will reveal itself as such when we try to read mythological details as if they were historical ones. We will then face unanswerable questions such as, "How could there be light and evening before the creation of the sun? How could a snake talk? How could a human body be made from dust? Who was Cain afraid would find him and kill him? From where did Cain get his wife? How could people live so long? How could the whole earth be flooded by enough water to cover the mountaintops?" But these questions are not unanswerable if one recognizes that the sacred author has simply used a mythological genre to tell this part of the story. They only become unanswerable if one insists upon reading the stories as they were never meant to be read.

Part of the task of interpreting the texts as the original hearers would have done involves acceptance of the scientific world as they understood it. Needless to say, their scientific outlook differed greatly from our own. This should not come as a great shock. We have known for some time that the ancients thought (for example) that the earth remained stationary and that the sun and the planets revolved around the earth. That is why Joshua commanded the sun to stand still in the heavens when he wanted to prolong the day (Josh. 10:12). Even today we speak of sunrise and sunset, even though we know that the sun does not in fact rise and set. But the ancients, looking at the sky, drew the obvious conclusions and thought that it did actually rise and set.

In addition to this, the ancients believed that people thought with their hearts, not their heads, so that the hearts beating in their chests were actually the organs in which thought originated. Emotions, on the other hand, were thought to originate in the kidneys. The God who tries and examines "the heart and kidneys" (in the King James Version of Ps. 7:9, "the hearts and reins"; in the Septuagint Greek, the *kardias* and *nephrous*) is the God who examines a man's plans and inner motivations. It does not matter that we now know that one's thoughts and plans come not from one's heart but from one's brain, and that the kidneys do not govern one's emotions and motivations but simply flush out bodily toxins.

Modern science bids us interpret such Bible verses in a poetical way. That is fine, but we must still recognize that for the original readers of these verses, the idea that one thought with the heart and felt with the kidneys was true both poetically and biologically. They actually believed that thought came from the heart and emotions from the kidneys or "reins." But what does it matter? The truth of Psalm 7:9 never did depend upon the accuracy of its biological presuppositions. Its sole point is not that thought and emotion come from the heart and the kidneys, but that God is the examiner and judge of both plans and motivations. We happily and correctly overlook the ancient science to focus upon the verse's real point.

We must continue to do the same thing when we read the early chapters of Genesis or any ancient Near Eastern literature. God does not teach science in Genesis 1 any more than He teaches astronomy in Joshua 10 or biology in Psalm 7. He *presupposes and condescends* to the science of the day to say what He has to say and to make His infallible and inerrant point. In reading the early chapters of Genesis, we do not look at the scientific presuppositions they make; we look *past* them to receive the true and abiding message.

If God had, for example, told Israel that the world was not stationary but revolved around the sun, such a teaching would have been pointless. They would not have been illumined but simply stunned and uncomprehending. And what would have been the purpose of offering such revolutionary science? Their immediate and urgent need was not to know about Copernican astronomy but about God's care and sovereignty. Given such urgent needs, God wisely decided to leave their science intact and tell His people what they needed to know.

Given the Israelites' hard hearts, such revelation was more than enough. It was all they could do to handle the lesson that the other gods were to be shunned. Their plate was too full to receive further lessons on the subject of cosmology. We moderns must therefore turn to the first chapters of the Bible with humble and teachable hearts. For a while, we must leave behind our world of microscope and telescope and laser. We come to the ancient Near East with the children of Israel, newly liberated from Egypt, and listen along with them, standing at the back of that trembling throng.

CHAPTER 1

The First Creation Story

Mankind as the Image of God

IN APPROACHING THE CREATION STORIES, we first need to appreciate what the concept of creation meant to the stories' original Israelite audience. For us post-Enlightenment moderns, "creation" means the bringing into physical concrete existence of something that before did not exist. "To exist," for us, means simply to be, to take up space in the universe. Something might have no name, function, use, value, or connection to anything else (for example, a piece of ruined rubble in an overgrown forest), but it would still be said to exist. We define existence in terms of physics.

It was otherwise for the ancients, including ancient Israel. For them existence implied function, connection, utility. If something had no organic and useful connection to the rest of society, and thus no name, it did not fully exist. Thus creation for the ancients involved not so much bringing objects into physical and material being as ordering their uses in a functioning society. We see this in the ways the Hebrew verb *bara'* ("to create") is used in the Scriptures—to denote not the act of making something from nothing (*ex nihilo*), but that of making it serve a particular purpose. Thus God created the heavenly beings and celestial realities for the purpose of praising Him (Ps. 148:1–5); He created the returning exiles for His glory (Is. 43:7), the destroyer to tear down (Is. 54:16), and Jerusalem to rejoice (Is. 65:18). This should prepare us to read the ancient and sacred text with an eye to function rather than to physics.

1 When God[1] began to create the heavens and the earth, [2] the earth was a desolation and emptiness, and darkness was over the face of the deep. And the *ruach*[2] of God[3] was moving over the face of the waters.

The first thing we notice in the creation story is the divine name *Elohim*. Though meaning simply "God" (a singular noun in the plural form), it is the word used throughout much of the Old Testament to describe Israel's deity, Yahweh. Indeed, in the second creation story in Genesis 2:4f, the name Elohim is paired with that of Yahweh, so that it is Yahweh Elohim who made the earth and the heavens.

Though it is fitting that a name as generically universal as Elohim should be used to describe the universe's creator, one should not miss the fact, obvious to the original hearers, that the text says it was the tribal God of Israel who created the world. Pagans reading the Babylonian *Enuma Elish* may have asserted that it was Marduk who set up everything and who was therefore the supreme deity. The Egyptians also had their own contenders for the role. But here, in the first three words of the Bible, we see that it was Elohim, the Hebrews' protector and God, who made **heaven and earth** (i.e., everything). The pagan deities had nothing to do with it. The

---

1   In Hebrew—*Elohim* (a plural noun, usually rendered as "God").

2   The Hebrew word *ruach*, which can mean either "spirit," "wind," or "breath," is left untranslated in the text to accommodate this variety of meanings (see commentary below).

3   Hebrew *ruach elohim*. One could conceivably translate *elohim* as a superlative ("a mighty *ruach*/wind"), but such usage would be unique in the Scriptures. The use of the word *elohim* in v. 1 to denote God strongly suggests that the word here refers to God and is not used as a superlative.

narrator polemically disdains and dethrones them by utterly ignoring them in his narrative.

The opening Hebrew words *bereshith bara' elohim*, usually rendered "in the beginning God created," is rendered here **when God began to create**. A similar syntactical construction is found in Genesis 2:4, and both seem to reflect the way ancient cosmological narratives began—with a statement of how things were before creation took place. (The *Enuma Elish*, for example, begins, "When above the heaven had not yet been named.") The sacred text is not concerned to locate the creation in time or before time. Its concern here is rather to glorify the Creator by stressing how hopeless things were in the earth before God created—namely, everything was **a desolation and emptiness**.[4]

The Hebrew words here translated "desolation and emptiness" are *tohu* and *bohu*, usually translated something like "formless and empty." The word *tohu* is often found in the Old Testament; the word *bohu* only occasionally, when it is paired with *tohu*—presumably for its rhyming value. When we turn from the usual translations of the term to see how the word is used (and therefore what it means), we see that the usual translations could stand some improvement. The thought of *tohu* is not "lacking in form," like a shapeless mass, but denotes its function (not surprisingly, given that creation for the ancients involved function). *Tohu* means "a desolation," "wasteland," "a useless, unproductive place." Thus the howling wilderness was tohu (Deut. 32:10), the idols which could not save or profit were tohu (1 Sam. 12:21), God caused His defeated

---

4   If one prefers the translation "In the beginning, God created the heavens and the earth," then these words will serve as an introductory summary for the entire account of creation beginning with v. 3, v. 2 describing the precreation chaos. The thought will not be much different from the one offered by the translation here, except for the additional assertion that God created "in the beginning."

foes to wander in a trackless tohu or wilderness (Job 12:24). When God made the earth, He did not make it to be tohu, but created it to be inhabited (Is. 45:18). When God judged Judah through the Babylonian invaders, He made the earth once again tohu and bohu—not a shapeless mass under water, but a wilderness, its cities laid in ruins and uninhabitable (Jer. 4:23).

Underlying all Old Testament usage of the word is the idea of utility, value, societal worth. The sacred text here declares that none of this existed before God began His work of creation. We miss the point if we insist on importing our modern concepts of creation and interpret the text as saying that the world was once nonexistent (as we define existence and nonexistence). The point here involves function—without God's involvement, nothing was any good, and life we as know it did not exist. There was no laughter or joy, no buying and selling, no wives and children, no sowing and reaping. Everything was desolate and unproductive, tohu and bohu.

Another way of describing such a state is to say that all was chaos, abyss, the sea, the deep, and moreover that **darkness was over the face of the deep**. It is just here that we are forcefully made aware that we are reading an ancient text. For if God hadn't begun to create, where did all this water come from? One could suggest that God created the heavens and the earth simply as a mass of water submerging the land in a state of primeval chaos, so that everything was created in a state of tohu and bohu. But scriptures like Isaiah 45:18 emphatically state that God did *not* create the world in a state of tohu, and anyway for the ancients creation and chaos were mutually exclusive.

In fact, the concept of everything before creation being a primeval sea and darkness is common in the mythologies of the ancient world. Once again we must remember that the ancients did not ask the questions we ask (e.g., how and what came into physical being first?). They were concerned with function. If all was sea and darkness, there could be no ordered world and no society. The sea and the deep therefore are a fit image for chaos, for tohu.

We find this, for example, in the opening verses of the Babylonian creation story of Marduk's supremacy, the *Enuma Elish*: "When above the heaven had not yet been named, and below the earth had not yet been called by a name, when Apsu primeval, their begetter, Mummu and Tiamat, she who gave birth to them all, still mingled their waters together . . . at that time the gods were created within them."[5] In this long epic, Apsu was the primordial sweetwater ocean, Tiamat the saltwater sea, and Mummu the mist arising from them.[6] Before the world was made, all was sea, the waters of the deep.

We find the same picture in another such creation story. That one begins, "A holy house, a house of the gods in a holy place, had not been made, a reed had not come forth, a tree had not been created, a brick had not been laid . . . all the lands were sea."[7] The ancients therefore would not have thought that the words "darkness was over the face of the deep" referred to the *created* waters, but to the abyss *before* the creation, the deep that lay in the darkness, awaiting creation's light. The darkened deep referred to the primordial chaos that God would have to overcome.

Faced with such chaos, God begins His work, for we see **the ruach of God was moving over the face of the waters**. The word *ruach* of course can mean either "wind," "breath," or "spirit," according to context. These meanings were based on the common observation that a person with breath was alive and had spirit.

---

5   *Enuma Elish*, tablet 1, lines, 1–9, in *The Babylonian Genesis*, by Alexander Heidel, Chicago: University of Chicago Press, 1942, p. 18.
6   Ibid, p. 3.
7   Ibid, p. 62.

Breath/ruach also refers to the movement of air, not only in human beings, but also throughout the earth, in the form of wind. We see this multiplicity of meaning in such scriptures as Ezekiel 37:8–10, in which the prophet is bidden to summon the ruach (i.e. the wind) to come from the four winds into the bodies of the dead to give them breath so that they may have spirit and life. The bodies had sinews and skin, "but there was no ruach in them. Then [God] said to me, 'Prophesy to the ruach; prophesy, son of man, and say to the ruach, Thus says the Lord GOD: Come from the four *ruachoth*, O ruach, and breathe on these slain, that they may live.' So I prophesied as He commanded me, and the ruach came into them, and they lived." The word *ruach* here combines all three meanings of breath, wind, and spirit.

We see a similar multiplicity of meaning in Psalm 104:29–30: God takes away ruach (here usually rendered "breath") from His creations, and they die and return to the dust. When He sends forth His ruach (here usually rendered "Spirit") like a wind sweeping through the earth, they are created, and He thereby renews the face of the ground.

This illustrates the difficulty involved in choosing a single word to translate *ruach* and the advantage of sometimes leaving it untranslated. God's ruach is His life, the power He sends forth to enliven His creation and give them breath. It was this very life-giving ruach that He sent to move upon the primordial waters of chaos. It came on the deep like a wind, full of God's power and force and Spirit. Later Christian Trinitarian theology would identify this ruach with the Holy Spirit, the Third Person of the Holy Trinity. This was not wrong but should form no part of our primary exegesis or be read back into the present text. The text here simply says that God's power, a wind sent from Him, filled with His supernatural and life-creating power, was **moving over the face of the waters**.

(We will see the same ruach from God push back the floodwaters of chaos in Genesis 8:1, and again in Exodus 14:21, where a strong ruach from the east drives back the waters of the Red Sea, allowing Israel to pass through and live.)

This life-giving movement of God's ruach forms the contrast to the tohu and bohu, the uselessness of the earth: even though the earth was desolate and unproductive, yet God's **ruach was moving over the face** of this primordial abyss, ready to create and bring order, utility, and beauty into being. The word rendered **moving** is also used in Deuteronomy 32:11, where it describes the action of an eagle hovering or fluttering over its young, and in Jeremiah 23:9, where it describes a shaking motion of the prophet's bones. The picture here therefore is that of the ruach of God circulating over the waters, moving, vibrating, ready for action. The earth may have been tohu and bohu, but God's power, like a wind over the water, was about to change all that.

Day One

> [3] And God said, "Let there be light!" and there was light. [4] And God saw that the light was good. And God separated the light from the darkness. [5] God called the light "day," and the darkness He called "night." And there was evening and there was morning, one day.[8]

---

8   That is, "the first day." Some ancient commentators, reading "one day" rather than "the first day," sought to find special meaning in the phrase, and suggested that the phrase "one day" spoke of the day as an image of eternity. In fact Semitic usage always counted things in terms of "one, second, third," etc. We see the same numerical usage in Gen. 2:11f—most English translations read, "the name of the first (river) is Pishon . . . the name of the second river is Gihon." The Hebrew literally reads, "the name of the one (river) is Pishon . . . the name of the second river is Gihon." In our text here, "one" simply means "first."

The change comes with a simple and sovereign word from God: **God said, "Let there be light!"** (in Hebrew, two short words, *yehi 'or*), **and there was light.** In the pagan mythologies, deities such as Marduk have to scheme and prepare and wage warfare to gain the victory and to create. The Hebrews' God was utterly different: He needed only speak a short and simple word of command in order to create. He in fact creates the entire cosmos by uttering a short series of ten commands (foreshadowing the Ten Words, or Ten Commandments), and His word is immediately obeyed.

The pagan mythologies often portrayed conflict and war of deity against deity before the world's order could be created. There is nothing like that here. None could gainsay the word of God. He needed only to say "Be!" and it came to pass. It is true that in addition to speaking, God performed the actions of making, separating, and setting (vv. 7, 16, 21, 25, 27), so that actions as well as words were involved. But the general picture is one of sovereign decree, like a king issuing orders from a throne.

What was God making when He created the light? All commentators have noted (some with chagrin) that the creation of light and of the day preceded the creation of the sun and the moon. Accordingly, some commentators have striven to find a factual scientific equivalent for this pre-solar light, one of them[9] saying that "this primeval light was probably electric, arising from the condensation and friction of the elements as they began to arrange themselves in order." The sacred text itself, however, is quite clear: this light was the daylight seen by all men when they woke up each morning. We see this in the name God bestowed upon the light, for He **called the light "day,"** separating it from the darkness, which **He called "night."** In other words, on the first day God created not a physical substance such as galactic light or electric charge, but *time.*

---

9   R. Payne Smith, in Ellicott's commentary, 1897.

The sacred text then says that God **saw that the light was good**. The narrator presents us with an image of God stepping back to look at what He had made, like a craftsman studying a newly made product to judge its quality. The divine Craftsman pronounced His product **good**. The word *good* (Heb. *tov*) here does not simply mean that physical creation is morally acceptable. In this context, the declaration and verdict of *good* means that the product of daylight would well serve its assigned function, which was that of allowing creatures to arise from the darkness of nighttime and live their lives. We can almost see a smile of satisfaction on the face of the divine Craftsman as He surveys His strong and beautiful created daylight.

The light being good and adequate to its appointed function, **God separated the light from the darkness**. That is, He did not claw apart the light from the darkness, but assigned to each their separate spheres of influence. Day would be followed by night, and daylight by darkness, as time began. Why does the text stress that God gave these things names? Because in the thought of the ancients, the conferral of a name bestowed function, and things did not truly exist until they were functionally related to society. Society requires that all things have names. Naming and **calling the light "day"** and **the darkness "night"** was essential to their full creation.

We see here now why light was created as the first of God's works, for time formed the foundation for the rest of creation. God created the first day, to be followed by the second, and so on for the entire first week. In creating daylight and time, God created the light in which He could work. Men needed light to work, and God also created the light and day during which He would continue to create the world.

After this, the period of a working day, **evening** came, ending God's labors as evening ended the labors of any working man. And then after this, the next **morning** came. This brought to a conclusion the work of the first day of God's divine work week. Mention of the first day marks the beginning of the structural outline of the creation story, that of the creation of the world in one week. Ancient Israel experienced working life in terms of weeks—in a single week a laborer, for example, could farm and harvest just so much. God did more than that: in a single week He created the whole cosmos.

Again we note that we must read this story as literature from the ancient Near East, which was concerned not with matter so much as with function—in particular, the functions of a world experienced through eyes unacquainted with our modern science. The ancients did not regard the sun as the sole source of light, since they experienced light even before the full sunrise. It did not confound them to think of daylight being created before the creation of the sun. It is a mistake, rooted in hubris, for us to insist that the Scriptures speak to us in conformity with our modern scientific understanding of the world. The sacred text spoke the language used by all the other ancient creation stories, that of poetry and metaphor—in other words, the language of mythology. A myth can be variously defined. Later New Testament usage, commenting on the myths of pagans and gnostics, would define a myth as a silly, untrue tale, unworthy of serious consideration (see Titus 1:14; 2 Pet. 1:16). Here *myth* refers to the way ancients told stories that tried to make sense of their world. In this definition, a myth is not an untrue tale but a story with a truth so big it cannot fit into a single historical event.

Realizing that the Genesis creation stories speak the language of mythology gives us the key to understanding things that might otherwise puzzle us. Were there really water and submerged land in the world before creation? Were there really daylight and nighttime and evenings and mornings before the sun was made? Did God really need light to work? Did He stop working when evening came? Was the whole world really created in six twenty-four–hour days? Discerning that Genesis uses mythological language enables us to hear what it is really saying. It is not teaching science or addressing itself to modern scientific questions. It is saying something much more important. It reveals that our God is the One who made everything and who presides over it all.

Day Two

> [6] And God said, "Let there be an expanse in the midst of the waters, and let it separate the waters from the waters." [7] And God made the expanse and separated the waters that were under the expanse from the waters that were above the expanse. And it was so. [8] And God called the expanse "heavens." And there was evening and there was morning, a second day.

On the second day, God said, **"Let there be an expanse in the midst of the waters, and let it separate the waters from the waters."** The word here rendered *expanse* is the Hebrew *raqia'* (sometimes rendered *firmament*, such as in the King James Version, from the Vulgate *firmamentum*). To understand this act of creation, we must recall that in the prior state of tohu and bohu, all was sea and deep waters. On Day One, daylight was created, but it came and went upon a submerged world. Here God brings order by making a dry space in the midst of the waters. He decrees that there be an **expanse** which would **separate the waters** below **from the waters** above. Obviously such an expanse would have to be solid in nature to hold up the waters above and keep them from all falling back down to the waters below. And that is just how the ancient Near East regarded the skies—as something solid.[10]

---

10   Hence the Latin translation *firmamentum* (compare our English "firm") and

This is clear enough from the rest of the Scriptures. In Ezekiel 1:22f, Ezekiel in his vision saw "the likeness of an expanse [Heb. *raqia'*]," shining like crystal, upon which stood God's throne. Obviously the expanse had to be fairly solid to support the divine throne. Job 37:18 describes the sky [Heb. *shehaqim*] as "hard as a molten mirror." Indeed, the noun *raqia'* comes from the verb *raqa*, "to hammer out." In Exodus 39:3 the verb describes the process of hammering out gold plate for use in the tabernacle shrine.

This solid sky is stretched out over the waters below (as a tent is stretched out; compare Ps. 104:2), keeping the upper waters away from the lower waters. It is in this space that all creatures will find room to live. The torrential rains of the Flood would come if the windows of this expanse were opened, allowing the waters above the expanse to fall through (Gen. 7:11). Those waters were kept at bay for now by the mighty solid expanse God made.[11] To complete its creation, God bestowed a name and **called the expanse "heavens"** [Heb. *shamaim*].

This part of the story would not have surprised any of the ancients, all of whom believed that an ocean existed above the clouds. Any creation story had to account for the separation of the waters down here in the sea from the waters above. Thus in the Babylonian *Enuma Elish* story, Marduk battled the primordial sea, personified by the chaos goddess Tiamat,[12] and split the sea apart into two halves: "he split her open like a mussel [or shellfish] into two parts; half of her he set in place and formed the sky as a roof. He

---

the Greek translation of the Septuagint, *stereoma*, from the Greek *stereos*, meaning "firm, hard, solid."

11   Even these waters had their part in the divine chorus of praise. Compare Psalm 148:4—"Praise Him, you highest heavens, and you waters above the heavens!"

12   We see cultural connections in the similarity of the name of the Babylonian goddess and the Hebrew name for the deep: Tiamat and *tehom*.

fixed the crossbar and posted guards; he commanded them not to let her waters escape."[13]

A comparison with ancient myths like the *Enuma Elish* shows not only how much Israel shared with its neighbors, but also how different were their faiths. Yahweh God had no need of ferocious combat against a rival deity, nor did He need to post guards. Even the untamable sea was no rival to His power. With a single command and sovereign act He separated the waters from the waters, and this life-giving separation persisted by His serene will alone.

We note in passing that the customary observation "and it was good" is omitted here, doubtless because the separation of the waters above from the waters below was of no functional use to society without the creation of dry land. Accordingly the declaration of goodness is delayed until the appearance of dry land on the next day.

Day Three

[9] And Elohim said, "Let the waters under the heavens be gathered together into one place, and let the dry land appear." And it was so. [10] God called the dry land "earth," and the waters that were gathered together He called "seas." And God saw that it was good. [11] And God said, "Let the earth sprout vegetation, plants yielding seed, and fruit trees bearing fruit in which is their seed, each according to its kind, on the earth." And it was so. [12] The earth brought forth vegetation, plants yielding seed according to their own kinds, and trees bearing fruit in which is their seed, each according to its kind. And God saw that it was good. [13] And there was evening and there was morning, a third day.

Continuing the work of making earth habitable on the next morning, **God said, "Let the waters under the heavens be gathered**

---

13   *Enuma Elish*, tablet 4, lines 137–140, in Heidel, op. cit., p. 42.

together into one place, and let the dry land appear." And it was **so,** for the waters obeyed the sovereign command of God. When the waters **gathered** themselves **together, the dry land** appeared from where it had been submerged. God gave them both their proper names, thus assigning their functions. He **called the dry land "earth,"** and the gathered waters **He called "seas."** Since this was now of some use, **God saw that it was good.**

There was more to do that day if the newly dry land was to prove productive. So then God said, **"Let the earth sprout vegetation,** that is, both **plants yielding seed, and fruit trees bearing fruit in which is their seed, each according to its kind."** Once again the earth obediently responded to the sovereign order, vegetation spontaneously sprouting from the now dry soil, with plants and fruit trees. The threefold repetition of the words "each according to its kind" shows the stability of the creation, for in the seed (stressed as being in both plants and fruit trees) was the promise of future growth and harvest.

Moderns concerned to fight against the theory of evolution have fastened on the phrase "each according to its kind" as a kind of slogan against evolutionary claims of the existence of transitional species. Whatever the value of such a battle, it is more important for exegesis to note that the point of mentioning stability of species and seed was to reassure an agricultural community. Life and prosperity through farming were only certain if what was sown would be harvested. Therefore the text stresses this certainty, assuring the farmers that if they planted wheat, they would harvest wheat, for everything would bring forth according to its kind. For the second time on this third day, God declared His work was good and would fulfill its function in society.

We pause to note three blessings for man that God has created thus far: time, weather, and food. The promise of stability and consistency echoes later in the Genesis stories, for after Noah's Flood brought back to the earth all the primeval chaos and overturned the original work of creation, God again promised man that he could depend upon receiving these three original blessings of time, weather, and food. After God smelled Noah's pleasing sacrifice, He promised, "While the earth remains, seedtime and harvest [i.e., food], cold and heat, summer and winter [i.e., weather], day and night [i.e., time] will not cease" (Gen. 8:22).

The first three days of creation were days of foundational blessing for all that was to come. The scene had been set, and the world was now ready to be filled with those eager to enjoy the blessings of time, weather, and food, as days one to three would be balanced by days four to six.

Day Four

¹⁴ And God said, "Let there be lights in the expanse of the heavens to separate the day from the night. And let them be for signs and for seasons and for days and years, ¹⁵ and let them be lights in the expanse of the heavens to give light upon the earth." And it was so. ¹⁶ And God made the two great lights—the greater light to rule the day and the lesser light to rule the night—and the stars. ¹⁷ And God set them in the expanse of the heavens to give light on the earth, ¹⁸ to rule over the day and over the night, and to separate the light from the darkness. And God saw that it was good. ¹⁹ And there was evening and there was morning, a fourth day.

Continuing His work of filling the world with all that mankind needed, on the fourth day **God said, "Let there be lights in the expanse of the heavens to separate the day from the night . . . and let them be lights in the expanse of the heavens to give light upon the earth."** We note this last detail—the great luminaries were to give light *upon the earth*, not outwardly to the skies. All of God's handiwork was created for us—for the animals and for mankind, who would live upon the earth. So, **God made the two great lights** as well as **the stars**. Though the stars were mentioned (how could anyone miss them, looking up at the sky at night?—at least anyone not blinded by urban glare), the main emphasis clearly falls here on the sun and the moon.

These lights are described as **the greater light to rule the day** and **the lesser light to rule the night**. It is clear why the narrator refused to use the usual terms for these lights (namely, the sun and the moon; in Hebrew the *shamash* and the *yarih*). For the pagan peoples, these were the names of gods, and the narrator did not want to give the impression that he was describing the creation of the sun god and the moon god (the *Enuma Elish* was replete with descriptions of such divine births). Such works as the *Enuma Elish* described the creation of gods in matter-of-fact terms, and our present author was determined not to give the impression that he was doing the same. The mighty sun therefore became in this narrative merely **the greater light** and the glorious moon merely **the lesser light**. He describes them as ruling the day and the night respectively, since "to rule" then simply meant "to preside over and to allow activity to occur." The sun and the moon therefore were not gods, but mere lamps, made to give light to the world.

They were also created **for signs and for seasons and for days and years**. The preposition **for** identifies three categories: (1) for **signs** (Heb. *othoth*), a distinguishing mark, which includes within it two subordinate categories: (2) **seasons** (Heb. *mo'adim*) and (3) **days and years**. The term **seasons** refers here to the cultic calendar of the feasts of Israel and all ancient peoples, and the term **days and years** also refers to the days of this calendar. The entire festal and cultic calendar of all the ancients depended upon such astronomical observations. The sun and moon therefore allowed men to observe a calendar of religious festal times.

The emphasis here falls upon the sun and the moon rather than the stars. We discern here a tacit rejection of the astrology so prevalent in the ancient Near East. Myths such as the *Enuma Elish* stressed the importance of the zodiac, but our story completely ignores it. The pagan gods such as Marduk may have stood in the center of the powerful zodiac, but in Israel the stars played little part. They are mentioned in passing, and even the sun and the moon are only mentioned as mere **lights**, **set in the expanse** to serve as illumination. They were not therefore gods, but mere lamps, like the simple lamps that give light to the houses of men. Note: they were not gods *to be served*, but merely lights *that served*. The word used to describe them is *me'or*, the same word used to describe the lamps of the Mosaic sanctuary in Exodus 25:6.[14] We discern here a quiet polemic, dethroning the gods and reducing them to mere furniture in the hands of Israel's Lord.

We also note a wonderful and poetic structural parallelism here. Just as on Day One God made the daytime and the nighttime, so on Day Four He creates the lights to illumine both the day and the night.

Day Five

[20] And God said, "Let the waters swarm with swarms of animate beings, and let birds fly above the earth on the face of the expanse of the heavens." [21] So God created the great sea-monsters and every animate being that moves, with which the waters swarm, according to their kinds, and every winged bird according to its kind. And

---

14 This suggests that the lamps of the Mosaic sanctuary image the cosmic luminaries, and therefore this sanctuary forms an image of the cosmic temple.

God saw that it was good. ²² And God blessed them, saying, "Be fruitful and multiply and fill the waters in the seas, and let birds multiply on the earth." ²³ And there was evening and there was morning, a fifth day.

As on Day Two when God separated the waters below from the waters above, so on this parallel round of creation on Day Five He created life both above and below, creatures to move in the waters and in the skies. By His sovereign command He made **the waters swarm with swarms of animate beings**, and **the birds fly above the earth on the face of the expanse of the heavens.**¹⁵ These creatures are described as **animate beings**, in Hebrew *nephesh hayya*, literally, those having a "living soul." In Hebrew the term *nephesh* or soul applies not to the divine likeness unique to mankind, but to all creatures that breathe and move and live.

We see here another instance of the verb *bara'*, to create, now used to describe the making of **the great sea-monsters**. The word here rendered **sea-monsters** is the Hebrew *tanninim*. We will miss the narrator's point if we translate the term simply as "whales" or "great sea creatures," as if they were just large fish. Ancient readers would have realized at once how extraordinary it was to regard God as the creator of the tanninim, for the ancients thought of these beings as liminal animals, beings living at the borders, creatures of chaos. In pagan mythologies they symbolized rebellion, and even in the Old Testament they still savored of menace. The terrible Leviathan was one of these creatures, as was Rahab (compare Job 3:8; 41:1f; Ps.

---

15 We note in passing the same anthropocentric view as we saw in the creation of the heavenly lights in v. 15. The lights of heaven were there described as giving light "upon the earth," and here the birds are described as flying "on the face of the expanse of the heavens"—i.e. across the expanse as one looks up from the earth to heaven. God makes the world primarily *for us*; mankind is at the center of His purposes.

89:10), and God warred against them (Ps. 74:14; Is. 27:1; 51:9).

Here the narrator declares that even these creatures are simply another part of God's handiwork. Unlike in pagan Near Eastern mythologies, they are not God's rivals or foes. God has no rivals. Even the terrible tanninim of the deep were made by God and form part of His world. Nothing in the world can be considered as on the edges of His sovereignty. He rules over all, and His care keeps harmony throughout the cosmos. The sea, considered a liminal place of chaos by most, was simply another place where His creative love could be seen.

With the creation of animate beings teeming in the waters and flying across the face of the firmament, God speaks for the first time directly to His creation, and it is a word of blessing. He **blessed them** (i.e., bestowed upon them life, vitality, fertility) and commanded them to manifest this blessing by being **fruitful**. They were to increase in number and **fill the waters in the seas** and **multiply on the earth**—even the dreaded tanninim! The terrible Leviathan, dreaded by mankind as the fearless king over all the sons of pride (Job 41:34), was simply another part of God's harmonious whole, created to play in the waters (Ps. 104:26).

Day Six

24 And God said, "Let the earth bring forth animate beings according to their kinds—animals and creeping things and living things of the earth according to their kinds." And it was so. 25 And God made the living things of the earth according to their kinds and the animals according to their kinds, and everything that creeps on the ground according to its kind. And God saw that it was good.
26 Then God said, "Let us make Man in our image, after our likeness. And let them rule over the fish of the sea and over the birds of the heavens and over the animals and over all the earth and over

every creeping thing that creeps on the earth."

²⁷ So God created man in His own image,
in the image of God He created him;
male and female He created them.

²⁸ And God blessed them. And God said to them, "Be fruitful and multiply and fill the earth and subdue it, and rule over the fish of the sea and over the birds of the heavens and over every living thing that creeps on the earth." ²⁹ And God said, "Behold! I have given you every plant yielding seed that is on the face of all the earth, and every tree with seed in its fruit. You shall have them for food. ³⁰ And to every living thing of the earth and to every bird of the heavens and to everything that creeps on the earth, everything that is an animate being, I have given every green plant for food." And it was so. ³¹ And God saw everything that He had made, and behold!—it was very good. And there was evening and there was morning, the sixth day.

The structural parallelism is maintained, for just as on Day Three God created the dry land, so on Day Six He fills it with animals and men. Before, the earth spontaneously sprouted vegetation and the waters spontaneously produced sea-creatures, and now **the earth** spontaneously **brings forth animate beings according to their kinds**. The phrase **animate beings** found in Genesis 1:20 is in Hebrew *nephesh hayya*, and it here refers to all the animals found on the earth—**animals** such as sheep and cows and oxen, **creeping things** such as lizards and locusts, and other **livings things of the earth**, referring to wild animals incapable of domestication. Like the fish and the birds, they were made **according to their kinds**, with a consistent stability that would allow animal husbandry.

As with everything else He created, God looked at His handiwork and **saw that it was good**, fully able to fulfill its function. Animals, especially wild animals, were often in that day thought to be dangerous and a threat to human existence. In this vision, everything is harmonious and works together to fulfill God's purposes—even the wild animals and earth's creeping things, even the lion and the viper.

Then comes the final act of creation, its culmination and crown. God said, **"Let us make Man in our image, after our likeness, and let them rule over the fish of the sea and over the birds of the heavens and over the animals and over all the earth and over every creeping thing that creeps on the earth."** The authority given to Man was total, for he was to **rule** over fish and birds and cattle and whatever crept on the earth. No living thing was excluded from the gift of human sovereignty.

Commentators have long noticed the plural in which God speaks: **"Let _us_ make Man in _our_ image, after _our_ likeness."** To what does this refer? Some have suggested that it reflects the fullness of the Godhead (also reflected in the plural noun _elohim_ when used as the divine Name)—a fullness that found ultimate fulfillment in the Trinitarian nature of God. Theologians who find in the Old Testament prophetic foreshadowing of Christian realities may justly claim this as one of them. But primary exegesis still asks what this plural would have meant to the original hearers of the text in the ancient Near East. And it seems too difficult to deny that they would have found in the plural usage a reference to the divine heavenly council.

All of the gods of the pagan nations lived and worked as part of a divine council, a heavenly pantheon. Of course Israel's intensely monotheistic faith would not allow for the existence of a pantheon of gods other than Yahweh, but it did retain an echo of the concept of God in council in the form of Yahweh's heavenly council with whom He discussed and communicated. Thus we read in 1 Kings 22:19–22 that, before arranging that King Ahab perish in battle at

Ramoth-Gilead, Yahweh asked for help from His heavenly council of angels. One of the angels volunteered to go and be a lying spirit in the mouth of the false prophets, enticing Ahab to join the battle. We find this divine council again in Psalm 89:5, where Yahweh is described as praised "in the assembly of the holy ones," which is probably why His abode is referred to as the "mount of assembly" in Isaiah 14:13. The angels, the sons of God, stand about Him (Job 1:6; 2:1), and they were present at the creation of the world and shouted for joy (Job 38:7).

It was as part of this council that Yahweh spoke when He asked the question, "Whom shall I send, and who will go *for us?*" and was answered by Isaiah (Is. 6:8). Psalm 29:1 urges the members of His council (lit., "sons of gods," *bene elim*) to ascribe to Yahweh glory and strength. For the ancient Israelite readers, nothing would be more natural than the thought of their Lord speaking and ruling from within a heavenly court. It is God in whose image Man is made (just as it is Yahweh who sends Isaiah in Is. 6:8), but He speaks in the plural as ruler of His heavenly council.[16]

We must also examine the question of what it means to be made according to God's **image and likeness** (in Hebrew, his *tselem* and *demut*). Once again we must extract ourselves from the Hellenistic mindset and reenter the Hebrew world of the ancient Near East. The terms "image" and "likeness" are here used more or less interchangeably,[17] but the emphasis clearly falls on the former term, since it alone is repeated twice in the next verse.

---

16 The plural "in our image" does not mean that Man is equally made in the image of the angels. In the question posed in Isaiah 6:8, Yahweh asks "Who will go for us?" but Isaiah is still considered the messenger of Yahweh, not of His angels. The heavenly council always remains in the background, and by the time Isaiah 40:14 was written the heavenly council, always culturally vestigial at best, had utterly faded from view. From at least the time of the Exile, the angels were seen to occupy a radically subordinate place.

17 If difference and nuance are to be sought, one may say that the addition of

In that ancient world, an image was a physical model of something—in the Old Testament, usually a model or statue of a pagan god, an idol (thus its usage in such passages as Num. 33:52, where Israel is commanded to destroy all the carved images and molten images of the pagans when they invade Canaan). In the pagan thought of the ancient Near East, the deity's work was done through its image and in some measure partook of the deity's essence. The image was not a reminder of an absent deity so much as the deity *was present through its image*. That is why kings in that culture set up statues of themselves where they wanted to establish their authority.[18]

We can see now what it meant for God to declare that He would create Man in His image—Man (in Hebrew, *adam*[19]), both male and female, partook of God's authority. Man, both male and female, would rule the earth as God's vice-regents, exercising the authority of the heavenly God as His stewards on earth. The bestowal of image referred not to any interior endowment, such as free will, the capacity for self-transcendence, or reason, though of course such endowments could be presupposed in anyone tasked with being His image on earth. The bestowal of the divine image was a gift of authority, which is why God immediately added that

---

the word "likeness"/*demut* safeguards the divine transcendence: "Whereas the image of the deity is equated with the deity itself in the ancient Near East, the word *likeness* serves to clearly distinguish God from humans" (Waltke, *Genesis, a Commentary* (Grand Rapids, MI: Zondervan, 2001), p. 66. We are not divine but a mere likeness of the divine.

18 Walton, John H., NIV Application Commentary, *Genesis* (Grand Rapids, MI: Zondervan, 2001), p. 130.

19 The word *adam* denotes both the human species and, later in chapter 2, a male individual. In this it parallels the English word "man" prior to the recent rise of feminist canons of political correctness. Until recently the word "man" was used to describe both the human species and the male of the species; thus the prayer in the Anglican Prayer Book "for all conditions of men" concerned itself with all human conditions and needs.

Man must rule over the fish and the birds and the cattle and indeed over all the earth. Ruling was how Man fulfilled his role as one created in the divine image. So, as soon as Man was created, God told him not only to be **fruitful and multiply**, but also to **rule**.

This was an astonishing notion in the ancient world and quite revolutionary. In the pagan creation stories, the gods made men to be their servants, to feed them and to do the work they had tired of doing. Men were created to feed their gods with sacrifices, to keep and clean their temple homes, to till the fields the gods no longer wanted to till.[20] *Kings* might be described as being in the image of the gods and partaking of their authority, but not the average laboring *man*—and certainly not the average laboring *woman*. Yet the Genesis story declared that every man and woman in the field and by the mill was created to rule the earth in God's name and partake of His authority. It was a breathtaking challenge to the cultural status quo. It elevated the humble and common person to a hitherto unimagined height and democratized the *imago dei*. Each person walking the earth had a dignity no one had dreamt of.

After creating *adam* in His own image, both the man and the woman, God blessed them. To bless meant to confer vitality and fertility. If a man and his wife were blessed, their children were as numerous as olive shoots around their table (Ps. 128:1–3); if a farming family was blessed, their garners were full, their sheep brought forth thousands and tens of thousands in their fields, their cattle were heavy with young and suffered no failure in bearing (Ps. 144:13–15). Thus when God blessed the newly created *adam*, both male and female, He said to them, **"Be fruitful and multiply and**

---

20 Compare *Enuma Elish*, tablet 6, lines 7–8: "I will create Man; upon him shall the services of the gods be imposed that they may be at rest," and lines 33–34: The gods "created mankind; he [the god Ea] imposed the services of the gods upon them and set the gods free."

fill the earth and subdue it and rule." We note here that fruit-fulness (i.e., sex) is inextricably linked with the image of God: it is because God made *adam* both **male and female** that they could be fruitful and multiply. They could **subdue** the earth because they had first **filled** it. Their functioning as God's image—ruling and subduing the earth—depended upon their first multiplying and fill-ing the earth. Sexuality is thus not foreign to the divine image in *adam* but foundational to it.

The ruling and subduing of the earth, however, did not imply force or violence. Some moderns have criticized the Genesis narra-tives for laying the foundation for the industrial rape of the earth and the selfish depletion and exploitation of its resources. However blame for such injustices and abuses may be apportioned, no one may justly lay such blame at the door of the Genesis narrator. The verbs denoting ruling and subduing (Heb. *radah* and *kabash*) do not imply violence or exploitation. The verb for *rule* [*radah*] is the same verb used when a shepherd rules his flock (Ezek. 34:4) or a king his dominions (1 Kin. 4:24). It can be done harshly and with force or lovingly and justly. Man is called to subdue the land in that he is to till and keep it (Gen. 2:15), bending it to his will and making it fruitful and safe from thorns and thistles. Man received the world as a gift from God, and like a good ruler he was called to protect and nurture it. As we will learn in the second creation story, *adam* (mankind) has the *adamah* (the ground, the soil) as his natural eco-logical partner.

In blessing Man, God gave the gift of food. With the word **behold!** He showed them the whole world that He had made (one can almost see the wave of His hand as He shows them the world) and offers it to them as their sustenance. To human beings and to all the animals, God gave **every green plant for food**. The image is one of primeval harmony; carnivores are nowhere in sight.

The narrator sums up the story of creation by saying that **God saw everything that He had made,** and it was not just good, but **very good.** This declaration of emphatic goodness and usefulness is preceded by **behold!** as if inviting everyone to wonder in amazement at the greatness of God's handiwork. Such a wonderful day, containing as it did the making of God's vice-regents and creation's stewards, is described not simply as "a sixth day" (as the other days were described with the indefinite article), but *the* **sixth day.** This was the day no one would ever forget.

Day Seven

2 And the heavens and the earth were finished, and all the host of them. ² And on the seventh day God finished His work that He had made, and He ceased on the seventh day from all His work that He had made. ³ And God blessed the seventh day and sanctified it, because on it God rested from all His work which in creating He had made.

Then the narrator reaches his climax on Day Seven. At last **the heavens and the earth** (i.e., everything) **were finished,** and **all the host of them.** The word **host** is the Hebrew *sabah.* It is the usual word for "army," and in the plural it forms part of an almost technical title for God: Yahweh is *Yahweh Sabaoth,* "the Lord of Hosts," king of the heavenly armies of angels. One catches a glimpse of their glory in the stars, and the phrase "heaven and all their hosts" (e.g., in Ps. 33:6) refers to the stars shining in the night sky. But the phrase "the hosts of the earth" is nowhere found. What can the use of the term *sabah* here mean?

The term seems to mean that just as the glory of a king is reflected in his vast army, so the glory of God is reflected in His vast creation, not just of the sun, moon, and stars, but of everything upon earth as well. A "host" is an organized, disciplined body of men (like an army), and all the created cosmos stands in organized harmony, reflecting God's order just as an army does.

By **the seventh day** God had **finished His work that He had made** on the previous six days, and so **He ceased on the seventh day from all His work that He had made**. There are two Hebrew words denoting work: one is *melaka*, describing the skilled work of a craftsman, and the other is *abodah*, describing the raw labor of the unskilled working man. Not surprisingly, the former word is used here (three times), for God had created the world with consummate skill and wisdom.

It is important to understand the statement that God **ceased on the seventh day from all His work**. If we think like moderns (and overworked moderns at that), we can misunderstand this cessation as God simply dropping His shovel and walking away from His creation job site to retire back to His place in heaven. This fails to see that the sacred text regards the cosmos as God's temple. In the creation stories of the ancient Near East, after the deity created, he rested by taking up residence in his temple and from there continuing to oversee the creation. In the *Enuma Elish*, for example, after creating the world the deity says, "Come, let us make something whose name shall be called 'Sanctuary.' It shall be a dwelling for our rest at night. Come, let us repose therein! There let us erect a throne dais. On the day that we arrive, we will repose in it."[21] God's cessation of labor narrated here was the prelude not to His departure from earth, but to His taking up residence in His temple—that temple being His newly made creation. This would be all the clearer to ancient readers, since each temple was considered a microcosm of the world.

The action of God's blessing and sanctification of the seventh day

---

21   *Enuma Elish*, tablet 6, lines 51–54, in Heidel, op. cit., p. 48.

referred to His taking up residence as king over creation, resting in His cosmic temple. This would have been easier for the ancients to discern than for us. Those cultures knew of a seven-day period as a preparation for God resting in His temple. For example, in Ugaritic mythology, Baal constructed his temple over seven days; at the Babylonian New Year festival, the god made a procession from outside the city before entering into his temple on the seventh day; in Sumerian literature we find the dedication ceremonies for a temple lasted seven days; and of course the Temple of Solomon was dedicated with sacrifices lasting seven days (1 Kin. 8:65).[22] The original readers of this story would naturally have regarded the seven days of creation as a prelude to the dedication of God's temple and His assuming residence there.

It is significant that **the seventh day** is nowhere here called "the Sabbath." That is because the term "Sabbath" inevitably referred to the Mosaic institution of rest in Israel, and that cultic obligation did not exist at the beginning of the world. The sacred text here says that *God* kept the seventh day; there is no suggestion that He then commanded mankind to keep it. Nor is there a shred of evidence in the Scriptures to suggest that Adam, Noah, or any of the Patriarchs ever kept the Sabbath. Whatever its cultural precedents in the ancient Near East, the Sabbath for the people of God made its first appearance as part of the Ten Commandments, given to Moses at the foot of Mount Sinai. At this later mandate, God rooted the Sabbath's significance in His primordial rest, as narrated here in Genesis and in Exodus 20:8–11. When Israel kept the Sabbath, it thereby acknowledged God's sovereignty over creation. They entered into a kind of temporal temple, joining God as He rested from His work of creation and took up His task of governing the world as its king. But the text here in Genesis describes

22 Walton, *Genesis*, op. cit., p. 155.

THE FIRST CREATION STORY

the roots of this later Sabbath, not its institutional and cultic establishment.

The Six Days of Creation and Modern Science

Perusing the first creation story of Genesis, it is clear that we are reading literature from the ancient Near East, for it shares the same cosmology as other creation stories from that time. We see the same dark watery abyss of chaos before creation, the same observational approach to the world. The ancients observed the physical phenomena in the world around them and concluded that there was a sea above them, for from where else could all that rain come? And they concluded that the sky must be solid, for how else could the liquid rain be held aloft when it wasn't raining? In other words, the ancients held what we could call (perhaps a bit condescendingly) a prescientific approach to the world.

God, in inspiring and moving the narrator of the Genesis creation stories, was not concerned to correct the ancient cosmologies the narrator inherited from his culture, nor to give lessons in science. The Scriptures were content to let the ancients keep intact their prescientific cosmology and other ideas (such as their belief that man thought with his heart rather than with his brain). The Scriptures had other concerns, and more important ones.

Our modern problem as Christians comes when we try to import our scientific understanding back into the Bible and impose upon the ancient text our own modern cosmology and science. We assume that for the Scriptures to be "true" they must be true to modern science and conformable to all the scientific advances made since the time of Moses. Though even here we are inconsistent, for we have no problem interpreting a text that declares man thinks with his heart as a poetic statement and not a medical one, but we have difficulty interpreting the creation stories with the same generosity of spirit.

We need not fear the theories of those suggesting some kind of evolutionary process was involved in our past, nor draw up to the battle lines when greeted by their pronouncements. These theories and pronouncements may or may not be true,[23] but even if they are true they have nothing to do with our interpretation of the sacred texts. Scientists validly concern themselves with scientific facts (and should resist drawing religious conclusions from them). Such scientific concerns are not those of the Scriptures.

Further, when we insist on interpreting the creation stories as if they were modern descriptions of the making of the cosmos and not as ancient poetry, we are in danger of missing their true and abiding lessons. These Scriptures do not teach science but something more fundamental. What things are those? I would like to briefly touch on eight of them.

1. Creation Is by Divine Plan

First, these early creation stories teach that the world exists and functions only because God first created it. That is, the world came into being not by random chance, but by the deliberate and loving decision of a Person. Often secular people assume there must be life somewhere else in the universe, because it seems to them too unlikely that the random chance which produced life on earth would not have produced it somewhere else as well. This assumes that life occurred on earth as a result of chance and not by decision or divine plan. The creation story here declares that random chance had nothing to do with it. If there is life elsewhere in the universe,

---

23 I myself am of a skeptical mind. I remember the counsel which C. S. Lewis once gave to theological students: "I do not wish to reduce the skeptical element in your minds. I am only suggesting that it need not be reserved exclusively for the New Testament and the Creeds. Try doubting something else." The quote is from his "Modern Theology and Biblical Criticism," in *Christian Reflections* (Grand Rapids: Eerdmans Publishing Co., 1973), p. 164.

it only exists there for the same reason it exists here—because our God decided to create it there.

The teaching that God created the world affects everything, and especially the issue of how we live. If everything came about by chance, then what we call ethics and morality have little meaning or validity. As Dostoyevsky's character Ivan Karamazov declares, "If there is no God, then everything is permitted." But if there is a God who created all things and if we only live because He created us, then mankind's common moral insights and intuitions retain some validity. The Scriptures portray God not only as a Creator but also as a Lawgiver, as the One who not only made us but also gave us the gift of conscience. The ten creative words in the Genesis narrative (rendered as "God said" in Genesis 1:3, 6, 9, 11, 14, 20, 24, 26, 28, 29) find their echo and fulfillment in the Ten Commandments.[24]

2. Creation Is a Gift

Secondly, these creation stories teach that literally everything we have and enjoy is a gift graciously given to us by God. Every breath we draw, every dawn and sunset we behold, every smile that lights up our heart, every piece of chocolate and every glass of wine—all comes gift-wrapped from God. The whole world is sacramental in that it points back to Him and invites our thanksgiving. Reading the creation stories aright kindles divine praise within us and reveals doxology as the basis of all authentic human existence. Man is not fundamentally *homo sapiens*, delighting in his own wisdom, but *homo adorans*, delighting in the grace and gifts of the Creator.

---

24 In Exodus 34:28 the Ten Commandments are literally "The Ten *Words*" (Heb. *dabarim*; Septuagint Greek *remata*).

3. *The Creator Is God Revealed to Us*

Thirdly, these Scriptures declare that the One who made the world is also the One who revealed Himself to us. His Name in the first creation story is *Elohim*—the name that is paired with *Yahweh* in Genesis 2:4. Our Creator therefore is Yahweh, the One who revealed Himself to Abraham (Gen. 12:1), who revealed Himself to Moses at the burning bush. "When Yahweh saw that Moses turned aside to see, Elohim called to him out of the bush, 'Moses! Moses!'" (Ex. 3:4). The Creator, Yahweh Elohim, did not retreat after creation to become the Deity of the deists, leaving the world to tick on by itself like a watchmaker's watch. He revealed Himself within the arena of history and eventually sent His Son to join us in that arena as one of ourselves. The creation narratives do not stand on their own but form part of an ongoing narrative, a story in which God continually and progressively reveals Himself to His covenant people. He is a God who invites us to know Him.

4. *Creation Is under God's Control*

Fourthly, these stories tell us that the universe is friendly. We do not live for an all-too-brief time and then find ourselves snuffed out, or go alone into the alone, trembling and helpless victims of a hostile and threatening universe. In the story of creation, God effectively conquered the chaos and brought everything into harmony. Now no corner of the cosmos is devoid of His care; nothing is beyond the reach of His sovereignty and love. Pagan religions did not reach such a height, and even Akhenaten's *Great Hymn to the Sun*, for all its sublimity, still left corners of the world dangerously divorced from the divine care. In praising the sun, the hymn says, "You [the sun] rest in the western horizon, and the land is in darkness in the manner of death. Every lion goes out from its den; every snake bites."[25] It is otherwise in the world our God made. All were made to live in harmony, and even the chaos-monsters like Leviathan found their part in this harmonious whole.

5. Man Bears the Image of God

Fifthly, we learn that every single human being bears the image of God and has been invested with the dignity that comes from being His representative in the world. Mankind is the crown of creation, the vice-regent of the divine, through whom God rules His creation. That rule is not one of oppression, coercion, or exploitation, but one of loving service and careful solicitude.

Since the establishment of Christendom, the idea that every human life is valuable is a given, but it was not so in the ancient Near East. At that time only kings were considered as bearing God's image or as being His representatives on earth; the common laborer had no such dignity. The Genesis creation story proclaims that even the lowest and humblest laborer bears the divine image. This teaching was not just revolutionary in ancient times. Even now, when we sell flesh through pornography and prostitution, and grind the faces of the poor, it is clear that we have not yet learned this lesson.

6. Male and Female Are Equal in Worth

Sixthly, Genesis teaches us that male and female are ontologically equal. Subsequent chapters will enlarge on the fruitful topic of gender roles, but here we learn that any gender differentiation does not negate a basic equality of worth between man and woman. The ancients found this a difficult lesson, and again we have not learned it even today. Wherever we find polygamy, or the reluctance to educate girls or to treat women with the same respect accorded to men,

25 *Hymn to the Sun*, in www.ucl.ac.uk/museums-static/digitalegypt/amarna/ belief.html

we find evidence that society has not hearkened to the first of the Bible stories.

7. Sex and Gender Are Built into Creation

Seventh, this creation story declares that sexuality is binary and fixed, and moreover that such a gendered existence is good. Past generations have wondered whether or not sex is good and have regarded it with suspicion. Our present generation opines that sex is not binary, nor is sexual gender a fixed reality, but that sexual identity and activity may be changed and altered to suit modern fancy. Standing against all such errors and delusions, both ancient and modern, Genesis declares once and for all, "Male and female He created them . . . and behold, it was very good."

8. Creation Reveals Christ

Finally, a Christian reading of the text will not fail to find Christological significance in the creation of *adam* in the divine image. Christians believe that the historical Christ was the incarnate and visible image, the *eikon*, of the invisible God (Col. 1:15). It is difficult not to detect in the first *adam* a prefiguring of this Incarnation. Our God is not a deity who forever hides Himself at a distance from this creation, remaining in splendid transcendent isolation in the heavens, revealing only His will to men who function as His lowly servants; He is a God who shares His authority with men. What God did in the first *adam* was but a prophetic sketch of what He would do fully and finally in Christ, the last Adam (1 Cor. 15:45). Adam shared the divine authority as a servant; Christ partook of that authority as a Son, so that everyone marveled that God had given such authority to men (Matt. 9:8).

These are the true and abiding lessons of the creation story. We need not fret if God chose to teach them while leaving intact the prescientific cosmology of His first audience. Those lessons provided more than enough for them to learn, even apart from learning about the intricacies of cloud formation and the meteorological existence of the jet stream.

Creation *Ex Nihilo*?

It appears from this sacred creation story that the world was *not* created *ex nihilo*, out of nothing, for prior to creation we see that water existed and even land, submerged beneath the water. It is possible that verse 1 ("In the beginning God created the heavens and the earth") described the creation of this material of water and land in a chaotic and unusable state, so that the water and submerged land existed because God had just created it in a jumbled form. But that is very unlikely and even contrary to the text itself.

As said above, creating in a state of chaos, where everything is tohu and bohu, would have been a contradiction in terms, as reflected in the clear declaration of Isaiah 45:18. Furthermore, the text speaks of God creating "the heavens and the earth"—that is, everything, not just water and land, but all things, both in earth and heaven. If we suggest that verse one narrates the creation of water and submerged land, then what about the creation of the sun, moon, and stars? For the text doesn't say that "God created the water and the land," but rather that He created everything—including presumably the sun, moon, and stars. We see therefore that the text will not allow us to insert a creation *ex nihilo* in verse one, but presents us with an already-existing watery chaos before creation.

This should not surprise us in as ancient a document as the Genesis creation stories. All ancient creation stories refer to this already-existing chaos and sea. That is because the ancients were singularly disinterested in the question of material origins. Rather, they were focused upon functionality and practical life. It was assumed more or less unreflectively that matter was eternal, and that was that.[26]

Our modern scientific age defines material existence in terms of *physical actuality*—whether or not something takes up space, regardless of its function in society. In this view, if a tree falls in a forest when no one is around, it still makes a sound. It was otherwise with the ancients who first read the Genesis stories. They defined existence in terms of *societal function*, and if something had no function in society, it did not exist in any sense worth discussing. That is why everything that existed did not merely come into being, but also *had a name*—the name by which its function in society was known. Given this understanding of the nature of existence (as functional, not physical), it is not surprising that the question of whether or not things existed prior to their functioning in society did not often arise.

The co-eternity of matter and deity of course depended upon a fairly low view of the gods, which is exactly what the pagans had (from the Jewish and Christian point of view). The pagan gods, even though able to create the world, still came into being as the children of other breeding gods; they could be killed and had to work and be fed. Given this understanding of the divine nature, it was not surprising to find the view that the gods were co-equals of matter and co-eternal with it. In Israel, however, there was from the start a different view of God and of His divine nature. God had no

---

26 There were some exceptions to this rule. As C. S. Lewis writes in his *Reflections on the Psalms* (London: Fontana Books, 1961), p. 69: "Admittedly we find in Plato a clear Theology of Creation in the Judaic and Christian sense. . . . But this is an amazing leap . . . by an overwhelming theological genius; it is not ordinary Pagan religion."

consort (as the pagan gods often did), no equal. He did not need sacrifices to thrive (Ps. 50:12–13 protests such a notion), He did not come into being through other gods breeding, and He cannot be killed. Such a revolutionary view of the divine nature could not fail to influence the question of creation.

Like their neighbors, Israel did not at first ask the question about whether or not matter had always existed, but shared with them a complete indifference to the question. That is why we read in the Genesis narrative about a watery chaotic abyss in a state of tohu before God began to create. But eventually Israel's exalted and sublime view of God's power and nature brought the question to the fore, and when that happened, they answered it by saying that of course God created the world out of nothing. We see this answer reflected in 2 Maccabees 7:28: "I beseech you, my child, to look at the heaven and the earth and see everything that is in them, and recognize that God did not make them out of things that existed." The ancients did not really understand the question about whether or not nonfunctional matter was eternal, and so they did not ask it. Their gods, weak and changeable as they were, gave them no incentive to inquire about the issue. But Israel's faith in their God's transcendent power did push them to ask the question and inquire.

In this sense, the resolution of the issue of creation *ex nihilo*, though not taught explicitly in the Genesis story, is present there in seminal form. The narrative speaks of precreation material, but the exalted view of God, present in both the Genesis narrative and the Hebrew Scriptures generally, pushes the reader to ask a fresh and revolutionary question and to answer it in a new way. Creation *ex nihilo* is present in the sacred text not as an explicit *teaching* but as a *trajectory*. The doctrine arises not from strict exegesis but as a fruit of meditation upon the uniqueness and power of Israel's God.

CHAPTER 2

The Second Creation Story

Mankind's Role in the Garden and Expulsion from It

This second creation story differs from the first one. Scholars have long noted the change of the divine name: in the first story the Creator is referred to as "Elohim," while in this second story the text refers to Him as "Yahweh" or "Yahweh Elohim" (or "Yahweh God"). This commentary does not speculate about earlier sources possibly used in the writing of the received canonical text, or about the relative value of identifying multiple authors of these sources. But it does seem that the use of a different name for God here witnesses to a separate creation tradition. In other words, it is unhelpful to try to harmonize this story with the preceding one and thus force the two tales to say the same thing. The two stories have different lessons to teach, and we must listen to them with humility and let the writer of this second story teach us as he wishes.

The name "Yahweh" refers more particularly to God's covenant dealings with His people, set in the flow of human history, and its use here moves us from the universal bird's-eye view of creation of chapter one to a more earthbound perspective. With the use of the name Yahweh, the reader moves from heaven to earth.

⁴ These are the generations of the heavens and the earth when they were created.

When Yahweh God made the earth and the heavens, ⁵ no shrub of the field was yet in the earth and no small plant of the field had yet sprouted, for Yahweh God had not caused it to rain on the earth, and there was no man to serve the ground, ⁶ but a flood was going up from the earth and was watering the whole face of the ground.

The phrase **these are the generations** (Heb. *toldoth*) will reappear another nine times in the Book of Genesis. The Hebrew word *toldoth* is related to the verb *yalad*, meaning "to beget, to give birth." The phrase "these are the generations" marks and identifies separate family histories. Thus the generations of Adam (Gen. 5:1) introduce the history of Adam's descendants; the generations of Noah (Gen. 6:9) introduce the history of Noah's descendants.

The phrase here denotes a more universal introduction—the account of what **the heavens and the earth** produced: namely, human beings and human history. It is also possible that we have here a polemic against the pagan creation mythologies of that day. In those mythologies, the gods begot other gods, who in turn became the heaven and the earth.[1] This is our writer's response to such stories—a reversal of the pagan order and a declaration that far from the gods begetting heaven and earth, the heaven and the earth begot human beings by the command of Yahweh.[2]

As in the first creation story, the narrator here contrasts what God created with the situation before He had begun His work.

---

1 In the *Enuma Elish*, for example, the primordial gods Apsu and Tiamat begot the gods Lahmu and Lahamu, and then the gods Anshar and Kishar. Eventually Marduk was born, who slew Tiamat, dividing her huge body and making from it the heaven and the earth (see Heidel, op. cit., pp. 3, 9).
2 As suggested by Walton, op. cit., p. 163.

Thus **when Yahweh God made the earth and the heavens, no shrub of the field was yet in the earth and no plant of the field had yet sprouted**. The terms **shrub** (Heb. *siach*) and **plant** (Heb. *eseb*) denote respectively the vegetation that grows wild and that which grows only with the cultivating help of man.[3]

What about the **flood** that **was going up from the earth and watering the whole face of the ground** prior to the rainfall or the creation of man? The word rendered here as **flood** is the Hebrew *'ed*, which some connect with the Akkadian *edu*, meaning "flood, swell, waves." It denoted groundwater arising from the subterranean ocean. In the ancient world, the soil was watered either by rainfall or by the inundation of rivers, which latter was brought to the plants through the labor of man in digging irrigation canals. In the time before God began His work on the land, there was neither rainfall (which would bring life to the shrubs of the desert) nor human labor (which would use the inundating flood from the underground waters). The result was no vegetation and no food. Thus before the creation of man, the inundating **flood going up from the earth** was of no use, and the earth remained unfruitful. Despite this water from the subterranean waters, the land before man was created was tohu; nothing grew upon the earth.

> [7] And Yahweh God formed the man of dust from the ground and breathed into his nostrils the breath of life, and the man became an animate being. [8] And Yahweh God planted a garden in Eden, to the east, and there He put the man whom He had formed. [9] And out of the ground Yahweh God made to sprout every tree that is pleasant to the sight and good for food. The tree of life was in the midst of the garden, and the tree of the knowledge of good and evil.

---

3   Thus Hagar found a *siach* growing in the desert (Gen. 21:15), but the man was created to eat the *eseb* of the field in his farming (Gen. 3:18).

A change from this unfruitful state came when **Yahweh God formed the man of dust from the ground**. There is a wordplay here in the Hebrew: the Lord formed the *adam* ["the man"] from the dust of the *adamah* ["the ground"].[4] That is, the ground formed the natural ecological partner of the man, the *adam*. God gave him the gift of the earth to till it and to bring food and life from it. The term **dust** (Heb. *apar*) means simply "dirt, soil, dust," but speaks also of man's humble origins. Though Yahweh will call the man to a tremendous dignity as His priest, he was created from the dust, which bids him remember his low origin and estate. The verb **formed** (Heb. *yasar*) is the same verb used for the potter forming the clay in Isaiah 29:16; it conveys the image of Yahweh as divine craftsman.

Having created this inanimate object, He **breathed into his nostrils the breath of life, and the man** [Heb. the *adam*] **became an animate being.**[5] Before Yahweh's divine inbreathing, the *adam* was simply a mass of dust or clay. But by God's own direct action, He **breathed into his nostrils the breath of life**. The verb **breathed** (Heb. *naphach*) denotes not a gentle blowing, but a vigorous puffing; it is the verb used for a smith blowing hard on the coals to make them glow (Is. 54:16) and for God angrily blowing away what rebellious Israel had stored up (Hag. 1:9). God thus created man with enthusiastic vigor. Though the man became an **animate being** like the animate beings/animals of Genesis 1:24, he differed from the animals in being created directly from the inbreathing care of

---

4   One rendering suggests that one might speak of God making an "earthling from the earth": Hamilton, Victor P., New International Commentary on the Old Testament, *Genesis 1–17* (Grand Rapids, Michigan: Wm. B. Eerdmans Publishing, 1990), p. 156.

5   In Hebrew, "a living *nephesh*," translated in the Authorized Version, "a living soul." A *nephesh* is something that breathes and thus is animated and able to move. The term is used in 9:15 to describe animals as well.

Yahweh Himself. The *adam* was no mere animal, but something created for a special and higher destiny.

Yahweh God not only formed the man but also **planted a garden in Eden, to the east, and there He put the man whom He had formed**. The word **garden** (Heb. *gan*) indicates something enclosed, fenced in (Heb. *ganan*); it is the word used to describe a royal park. This garden is described as being **in Eden, to the east**. The word **Eden** is derived from the Hebrew word for delight, pleasure[6] (the Septuagint Greek has *paradeisos*, "paradise"). The idea of Eden being **to the east** of the narrator seems to place Eden in the place of sunrise, of light, in the dwelling place of God. Here **the east** is not so much a direction of the compass as an indication of its location in the distant presence of God, far away from the mundane and normal.

In this garden God **made to sprout every tree that is pleasant to the sight and good for food**—that is, all that was needed to sustain the man in God's presence. There was no need to leave Him to find food or delight. There were two other trees there easily at hand:[7] the **tree of life** and the **tree of the knowledge of good and evil**. These will feature prominently in the coming narrative. The former tree denotes the source of immortality and life, while the latter denotes the claimed right to decide for oneself how

---

6   Compare Sarah's question in Genesis 18:12: "After I have become old, shall I have *edenah*/pleasure?"

7   The trees are described as being "in the midst [Heb. *betok*] of the garden," i.e., not necessarily in the mathematical center, but easily found, not hidden or on the fringes. The word is used when the man and wife hid themselves from God "in the midst [Heb. *betok*] of the trees of the garden" in Genesis 3:8, and when Noah was seen by his sons naked "in the midst [Heb. *betok*] of his tent" in Genesis 9:21. The Septuagint reads εν μεσω/*en meso*, which drew perplexity from such commentators as St. Gregory of Nyssa, who wondered how two different trees could both literally occupy the *exact center* of the garden at the same time (mentioned in his letter to Olympias as a preface to his commentary on the Song of Songs).

one should act.[8] Here the tree of the knowledge of good and evil symbolizes moral autonomy, the right to make moral decisions without reference to God—and thus God wisely forbids man to partake of it.

> [10] A river flowed out of Eden to water the garden, and there it
> divided and became four rivers. [11] The name of the one is the Pis-
> hon. It is the one that flowed around the whole land of Havilah,
> where there is gold. [12] And the gold of that land is good; bdellium
> and onyx stone are there. [13] The name of the second river is the
> Gihon. It is the one that flowed around the whole land of Cush.
> [14] And the name of the third river is the Tigris, which flows east of
> Assyria. And the fourth river is the Euphrates.
> [15] Yahweh God took the man and put him in the garden of Eden
> to serve it and guard it. [16] And Yahweh God commanded the man,
> saying, "You may indeed eat of every tree of the garden, [17] but of the
> tree of the knowledge of good and evil you shall not eat, for in the
> day that you eat of it you will surely die."

The garden is further described. **A river flowed out of Eden** into the garden, which was adjacent to it, **to water** the garden. After leaving the garden, the river **divided and became four rivers**. Two of the rivers, **the Tigris**[9] and **the Euphrates**, are well known. Despite the scholarly effort expended at determining the identity of the other two rivers, **the Pishon** (meaning "leaper") and **the Gihon** (meaning "gusher"), everyone acknowledges that certain identification is

---

8   Thus for example, in Deuteronomy 1:39 those children "who have no
     knowledge of good or evil" are those without the responsibility for making
     their own moral decisions.
9   Described here as being "east of Assyria," the ancient capital of the Assyrian
     empire. The term "Assyria" must refer to the capital and not the empire itself,
     because the Tigris does flow east of the *city*, but runs through the middle of
     the *country*.

impossible. The suffix "*-on*" seems to indicate a diminutive, rivers smaller than the mighty Tigris and Euphrates. Some scholars, identifying **the land of Cush** with Ethiopia or Nubia (its usual designation), favor an Egyptian provenance, and suggest the Pishon and the Gihon might be the Blue and White Nile. Others, on the basis of Genesis 10:8, identify Cush with the Cassites in western Iran and place the Gihon in Mesopotamia. Some identify the Pishon with the Halys River flowing into the Black Sea and the Gihon with the Aras River, flowing into the Caspian.

Fortunately the main point of the description does not depend upon identifying all four rivers with certainty. Eden is described as the palace of God. Kings often planted parks next to their royal residences, and here the narrator portrays Yahweh as planting a garden next to His Edenic residence.[10] The river that arose in Eden and flowed out of it is the river of life often associated with divine temples. We see this common motif reflected in Ezekiel's vision of the restored temple, where water issues from below the threshold of the temple and grows to become a mighty river giving life to all the land (Ezek. 47:1f). We see it in the Psalmist's poetic description of God's city, which is made glad by the streams of a river (Ps. 46:4). We see it in Zechariah's vision of the glorified city of God with living waters flowing from it (Zech. 14:8).

Since it was God's dwelling, naturally a river flowed from it, watering His garden and flowing from the garden to become four rivers, giving life to all the world. The narrator portrays all the world's rivers, such as the mighty Tigris and Euphrates, as finding their ultimate source in God's primordial presence and provision. The earth that was nourished by these rivers was a good and rich

---

10   Thus Walton, *The Lost World of Adam and Eve* (Downers Grove: IVP Academic, 2015), p. 117: such parks "were common accoutrements to temples and palaces in the ancient world."

earth, full of all that could be needed to adorn a temple—things such as **good** quality **gold, bdellium,** and **onyx stone.**

This is the significance of God setting the man **in the garden of Eden to serve it and guard it.** Eden and its garden was not just another piece of Near Eastern real estate, farmland somewhere in Mesopotamia. If the whole cosmos was God's temple, then Eden was the Holy of Holies, the epicenter of the divine Presence in creation, the primordial place from which all sanctity and life flowed.

God **took the man** He had made **and put him in the garden to serve** there as His priest and **to guard**[11] the sacred garden and keep it safe. Where sacred gardens existed in the ancient world, they were always tended by priests who cared for the trees and the animals in the enclosed park and preserved the sanctity of the enclosure. Thus the man's task in the garden was not so much one of mere farming as one of priesthood. This is reflected in the narrator's choice of verb: the man's job was **to serve** the garden (Heb. *abad*) and **to guard** it (Heb. *shamar*)—two words regularly used to describe the service of priests and Levites.[12] Serving and guarding the garden of course involved agricultural duties (the word *abad* is used in Genesis 2:5 and 3:23 to denote such duties of tilling and farming), but here it also denotes the sacred service of priesthood. The man was placed in the sacred enclosure not simply for landscaping duties but to tend the Holy of Holies in God's presence.

Yahweh allowed His servant to eat from the garden he was serving, generously offering **every tree of the garden.** Only one was off limits: God warned him **not** to **eat** of **the tree of the knowledge of good and evil.** We have seen that the eating of that tree constituted

---

11   The same verb is used in Genesis 3:24, where it describes the cherubim guarding the way to the tree of life and keeping the man and his wife away.

12   Compare Numbers 4:23, where service in the tent of meeting is termed *abodah*, and Numbers 3:7, where the Levites are instructed to guard [*shamar*] their charge, keeping the sacred vessels from profanation.

usurping the place of God, proudly arrogating to oneself the right to make moral decisions without reference to God. Such rebellion would destroy in man the living root of life, cutting him off from God, leaving him to wither and die. No wonder Yahweh in love forbade such a disastrous course, emphasizing the prohibition by adding a threat: **in the day that you eat of it you will surely die**.

The phrase **in the day** does not mean that within twenty-four hours of eating the fruit the man would keel over and die. The phrase is not an indicator of time, but of certainty. Thus in 1 Kings 2:37 David promised the rebel Shimei that "on the day" he left Jerusalem and went forth across the Kidron he would die. Obviously Shimei would not die on the actual day he departed, but later, after the king apprehended him. The term "in the day" here means "certainly." The threatened sentence of doom was no bluff.

> [18] Then Yahweh God said, "It is not good that the man should be alone; I will make him a helper fit for him." [19] So out of the ground Yahweh God formed every living thing of the field and every bird of the heavens and brought them to the man to see what he would call them. And whatever the man called each animate being, that was its name. [20] The man gave names to all animals and to the birds of the heavens and to every living thing of the field. But for man there was not found a helper fit for him. [21] So Yahweh God cast a deep sleep on the man, and while he slept took one of his sides and closed up the flesh in its place. [22] And the side that Yahweh God had taken from the man He built into a woman and brought her to the man. [23] Then the man said,
> "This one, this time, is bone of my bones
> and flesh of my flesh!
> This one shall be called *ishah*,
> because she was taken out of *ish*!"[13]

---

13 We have left the Hebrew untranslated to bring out more clearly the wordplay.

²⁴ Therefore an *ish* shall leave his father and his mother and cling to his *ishah*, and they shall become one flesh. ²⁵ And the man and his *ishah* were both nude and were not ashamed.

For the first time a note of discord is sounded. Until now everything that God had made was declared very good (Gen. 1:31). Now we learn that something in the world was *not* good—namely **that the man should be alone.** In the context of the creation stories, "good" (Heb. *tov*) means "functional, able to fulfill its appointed use in society." Thus in declaring that man's aloneness was not good, the narrator does not suggest that the man was lonely and required a soulmate to ease his pain. Rather, the narrator explains that if the man was to perform his functions of multiplying and subduing the earth and of caring for the Edenic garden shrine, he would require help. The declaration of "not good" refers here to the man's function, not to his psychological state.

His helper had to be **fit for him**—corresponding to his nature and need. The Hebrew term for *helper* is *ezer*; the term for *fit* is *kenegdo*. The term *helper* itself implies no inferiority on the part of the helper, for it is often applied to God, the great Helper of His people (e.g., Ex. 18:4; Ps. 70:5). The term *fit* here literally means "standing opposite," and it not only refers to the requirement that the man's helper must match him and correspond to him, but also carries nuances of complementarity.

Accordingly, **out of the ground Yahweh God formed every living thing of the field** (i.e., every beast; compare Gen. 1:30) **and every bird of the heavens and brought them to the man to see what he would call them.** The act of naming the creatures involved more than simply placing verbal labels upon them. It also

---

There are two Hebrew words in the text used for "man": *adam* (here rendered "man") and *ish*.

involved the man's recognition of their essential nature and thus of their potentiality (or otherwise) to become "a helper fit for him." This does not mean, of course, that the main goal of the help was simple companionship. One cannot sensibly conclude from such an ancient text that the offering of animals to the *adam* before the creation of woman meant that marriage was primarily about companionship and that sexual complementarity was irrelevant, so that as long as a man had company from a partner the gender of the partner was of no importance. Such a modern reading of the text would be staggeringly anachronistic. The introduction of animals as possible companions serves only to underscore their unsuitability and the divine wisdom in the creation of woman. It introduces and highlights the primordial irreducibility of mankind's binary and gendered existence. One must read these verses as part of the total flow of the narrative, leading up to the final ecstatic conclusion in the creation of the man's *ishah*.

We note in passing that the chronological order of the creation of the animals differs here from that in the first creation story, which related that the animals were created before the human pair was made. This is not a contradiction but simply evidence that the author of Genesis used two different stories, both complete with their own different lessons. More important is the narrator's portrayal of the man participating in the divine act of creation as God's co-creator. In ancient thought, the bestowal of names was an essential constituent to creation, for no creation was considered complete unless the thing made was assigned a name and function. Though Yahweh created the animals from the ground,[14] yet He delegated the final part of their creation to the man, giving him full authority to name them. These names were no mere verbal tags (as names are

---

14   Another difference from the first creation story, where in Genesis 1:24 the earth is to produce the animals spontaneously on its own.

in our culture) but referred to their assigned functions and natures in the world. The sacred text is emphatic about this astonishing delegation of creative authority: **Whatever the man called each animate being, that was its name**. Unlike in pagan mythologies, man is no mere laborer for the gods, but by God's will he acts in the world as His colleague.

The man faithfully obeyed God and gave names to all the animals on earth and birds of heaven, **but for man there was not found a helper fit for him**. Those reading these stories as history are somewhat nonplussed at the thought of God wondering if any of the animals might prove a fit helper for the man, and so they often suggest that God of course knew none of the animals would fit the bill, but nonetheless brought them to the man so that he might have this insight by experience as well. The ancients may not have read the text as if God's actions contained such a hidden agenda. Rather, the story served to emphasize the fundamental difference between the animals and the woman: it was found and discovered (by the man and Yahweh?) that none of the animals would serve the purpose of providing a helper fit for the man. Yahweh would have to provide something else, something completely different from the animals.

And Yahweh immediately took steps to provide this: He **cast a deep sleep on the man, and while he slept took one of his sides and closed up the flesh in its place**. This **deep sleep** (Heb. *tardemah*) was no normal or natural doze, but a supernatural coma and slumber to render the man senseless for the coming radical procedure. The word is used for the divinely caused sleep in Genesis 15:12, 1 Samuel 26:12, and Isaiah 29:10. This is significant, for it emphasizes that the man had absolutely nothing to do with the creation of the woman. He was in no sense her creator but was entirely passive during the entire operation. God alone created woman; the man simply provided the raw material. This reveals the dignity of the woman: she was as much the creation of God as was the man.

In the poetic description of woman's creation, we read that God **took one of** man's **sides** as the raw material for the woman. The word for **side** here is *tsela*, often translated as "rib." It is the word used to denote the side of the ark (Ex. 25:12) or the side of a hill (2 Sam. 16:13). In fact nowhere else in the Old Testament is *tsela* rendered "rib," and it seems this rendering was preferred because the translators balked at what the text actually implies—namely that Yahweh split the man in half and used one half for the creation of the woman. Such surgery would seem too radical to be historically accurate, and so the translators opted for God taking a single rib—a less radical medical procedure. But the text affirms that Yahweh took an entire side from the man—that is, half of him—to create woman. It was this side (or, if one prefers, this aspect) that God **built into a woman**. The word rendered **built** is the Hebrew *banah*, indicating that the resultant creation was strong, durable, lasting. It is the same word used in Psalm 127:1 for the laborer building his house.

Then came the dramatic moment of presentation. As Yahweh had brought to the man each of the animals, and it was discovered that none of them would suffice as a helper fit for the man, so He **brought** the woman **to the man** also. And here at last was what he was looking for! The man ecstatically exclaimed in discovery, "**This one, this time, is bone of my bones and flesh of my flesh!**" After so many failures, finally, **this time**,[15] success! The woman was his match, his other self, corresponding to him in every way, utterly different from the animals that had been brought to him—which is what the term **bone of my bones and flesh of my flesh** here means.

---

15 Rendering *happa'am* here as in Genesis 29:34 (thus Hamilton, New International Commentary on the Old Testament, *Genesis 1–17*, Grand Rapids, Michigan: Wm. B. Eerdmans Publishing, 1990, p. 177).

Such identity of essence involves a commitment to loyalty as well: when all the tribes of Israel told David they were his bone and his flesh, they did not mean they were related to him by blood. Rather they pledged their loyalty to him as if they were in fact related. In the same way, the man's exclamation that the woman is his bone and flesh can be seen as his pledge of love and loyalty to her.

The man was tasked with naming the animals, bestowing function and expressing his authority over them (v. 19). Coming hard on the heels of that, it is difficult to avoid the conclusion that by calling the woman something (*ishah*) the man was fulfilling this divine mandate and giving her a name as he before named the animals. Yet even so, this naming is not exactly on par with the dispassionate naming of the animals. It is also a cry of joyful discovery, a primordial *eureka!* as the man suddenly recognized in the woman a feminine mirror image of his own self. The actual and formal naming would come later, in Genesis 3:20. For now the man exclaims that she **shall be called *ishah*, because she was taken out of *ish*.**

The word *ishah* is the normal Hebrew word for *woman/wife*, just as the word *ish* is the Hebrew word for *man*. The wordplay is all the more wonderful, since the "-ah" ending of the word *ishah* is the usual feminine noun suffix. No matter that Hebraists deny any real etymological connection between *ish* and *ishah*—the wordplay serves to make the spiritual connection: a woman is the same as a man, only feminine. God brought to the man his true counterpart, and the man instantly recognized her as such.

The narrator closes with the cultural observation that because of such closeness, **an *ish*** (i.e., a man) **shall leave his father and mother and cling to his** own ***ishah*** (i.e., his woman/wife), **and they shall become one flesh**, a single organism. The verb rendered here *cling* is the Hebrew *dabaq*, the same verb used in Job 38:38 to describe how clods of earth stick together after the rain.

It thus describes no mere conjunction but a complete joining into one. Sociologically this statement seems problematic, for in Israel the woman left her family to join the man, not vice versa. But the statement should be regarded not as a sociological observation, but as a spiritual one—that is, the man's inner connection to his wife is stronger and more ontologically basic than his previous connection to his family—a mighty link indeed.

This description of the creation of the woman is remarkable when considered in the culture of its time. Ancient creation stories did not narrate a separate creation for woman but subsumed this topic under the creation of the man. Here woman is deemed worthy of separate consideration. The foundation has been laid for a theology most modern cultures have even yet not been able to internalize and express.

The story of the creation of the man and his woman concludes with the statement that they were **both nude and not ashamed**. All was innocent and good. The word rendered **nude** is the Hebrew *arom*. It contains hints of vulnerability—a vulnerability we will see exploited in the next chapter.

Learning from Adam and Eve

This second creation story offers certain lessons on human nature, gender, marriage—and even Christology. We can draw upon the text for these lessons because the text does not narrate the biographies of two individuals so much as the origins of two archetypes. We see this in the lack of proper names for the two characters: the male character is referred to simply as "man" (Heb. *adam*) or as "the man" (Heb. *ha-adam*). The female character does not yet have a name; she is referred to as "woman" (Heb. *ishah*) or as the man's *ishah* (i.e., his woman/wife).

By this reference to the male simply as "man," the archetypical nature of the story is accentuated, whereas it is obscured if the Hebrew for "man" is rendered as the proper name "Adam." It was thus not just the first *adam* who was made from the dust; *we all* were made from the dust (Ps. 103:14). It was not just the first *ishah* who was bone of her husband's bone and flesh of his flesh; every husband and wife are thus united as one single flesh. The archetypical nature of the story makes it more relevant to our situation, not less. The story of course reads as if it were a biography (all stories read that way, even allegories such as *Pilgrim's Progress* and the Lord's parables), but it speaks fundamental truths about the creation and nature of all men.

The first truth the story proclaims is the lofty nature of man/ *adam*. Though man is formed from the humble dust of the earth (and dust is always an image of humility; compare Ps. 103:14; 113:7), yet God made him with special care. God may have formed the animals from the ground, even as He formed man from the ground—the same words for both *formed* and *ground* are used in both Genesis 2:19, 7—but even so the man occupied an incomparably higher place. Even apart from the assertion of the first creation story that mankind (Heb. *adam*) was made in God's image (Gen. 1:26), we can see clearly from this second story that the man was special. Of no other creature was it said that Yahweh Himself blew into his nostrils to give it life.

Given the special care God lavished him, we are not surprised to see that God took him and placed him in His royal garden to tend it as His priest. Nor are we surprised to see man sharing with Yahweh in the creation of the animals by bestowing on them their names and thus establishing their functions on earth. This is the second creation story's version of *adam* being made in the divine image, for he is called to minister to God as a priestly intermediary between Him and His creation. In the words of the psalmist, God gave him dominion over the works of His hands and put all things under his feet (Ps. 8:6). Such authority brings with it responsibility to tend the world and protect it, as a king protects his people.

A second lesson of the story is that the man and his woman (to employ the terminology of the story itself; Gen. 2:25) are the ontological equal of each other. The first creation story expressed this by declaring that both the male and female were *adam* and made in God's image (Gen. 1:27); this story expresses that same truth through the man's ecstatic recognition that the woman was bone of his bone and flesh of his flesh, a feminine version of himself, an *ishah* from an *ish* (Gen. 2:23). This was a revolutionary thought in ancient times, when polygamy was allowed and women were treated like chattel. The widespread use of pornography, the flourishing of the sex trade and even sexual slavery, the common abortion of girls in some cultures, and the persistence of rape and domestic violence all prove that this continues to be a revolutionary thought in our own day as well.

Thirdly, this story shows that this ontological equality is compatible with male leadership in the family (or, if one prefers the term, with male headship). Whether here in Genesis 2:23 or later in Genesis 3:20, the man named his wife just as he had previously named the animals, indicating a measure of protective authority. Further, the man was made first and was the first to receive commands from Yahweh; the woman came afterward and learned of these commands through the man. Also, she was made to help him; he was not made to help her. In all these details we note a priority and preeminence bestowed upon the man (a priority noted by St. Paul in 1 Timothy 2:13f as he reflected on these passages). Man and woman are declared to be equal but different; of identical worth to God but having distinct and different roles. Ontological equality does not entail interchangeability.

Fourthly, this story declares that sex is good. There is no suggestion, either in the first or the second creation story, that sexuality and a gendered existence for humanity were in any way morally dubious, or even that they were created as a concession to sin, death, and the Fall. One can, of course, invoke God's foreknowledge and suggest that God only invented humans as sexual beings because He knew they would sin and die and thus need some way to continue the race. It is not clear that the question itself is meaningful. What is clearer is that the sacred text declares that everything God made was "very good," including gendered human beings with their sexuality. This means, of course, that sexuality is basic to human nature, and that sexual sins are more basic and the damage they do to the spirit within is more profound. That is why St. Paul would write that the fornicator by his fornication sins against his own body—in other words, his deepest self (1 Cor. 6:18). It also explains why sins of sexual perversion, sins "against nature," garner such condemnation from the apostle (Rom. 1:26–27). It is because sexuality is so good and so basic that its misuse is so devastating.

Fifthly, we note in the story the creation of a new reality, a new way of relating. Man and woman, while remaining distinct, were also one flesh, one organism. This allowed for a new kind of love, surpassing the love of neighbor. When a person loves his neighbor, he loves a separate individual, but in loving one's spouse, one also loves oneself, one's own flesh, for the unity of husband and wife transcends all the human unities, including the sacred unity of family (hence the man is said to leave his family to cleave to his wife). In this new unity, the dichotomy between I and Thou is overcome, and a man's bride can also be his own body. As St. Paul would later observe, this is no other reality than that of Christ and His Church, for the Church is Christ's bride and also His body (Eph. 5:29–32). This creation story contains for Christians a hidden *mysterion*, a revelation that can only be appreciated by those experiencing the reality of Christ in His Church. In this unity between the *adam* and his *ishah*, we see our own ecclesial story prophetically foreshadowed.

Finally, the story teaches us that human beings were created to function as God's priests in the temple of His creation. We see this insight also in the poetry of St. Ephrem the Syrian. In one of his hymns on Paradise, he wrote, "God did not permit Adam to enter that innermost Tabernacle; it was withheld so that he might first prove pleasing in his service in that outer Tabernacle; like a priest with fragrant incense, his keeping of the commandment was to be his censer; then he might enter before the Hidden One into that hidden Tabernacle."[16]

Even though Adam and his wife were expelled from the divine temple of Paradise and forfeited their priestly roles, the text abides as a revelation of the true vocation of humanity. A human being is by definition and calling a priest of God—a vocation returned to us by Christ through baptism, wherein all Christians are made part of the royal priesthood. The Church therefore functions as a microcosm of the world (even as church buildings functioned as microcosms of the created cosmos), a pledge of mankind's restored destiny in the age to come. Our original priesthood, lost through sin, is restored to us in Christ, and through that priestly ministry we Christians offer the world back to God through our praise, proclaiming the excellencies of Him who called us out of darkness into His marvelous light (1 Pet. 2:9).

3 Now the serpent was more shrewd than any other living thing of the field that Yahweh God had made. He said to the woman, "Really! God actually said 'You shall not eat of any tree in the

---

16 Hymn 3:16, in *Hymns on Paradise*, translated by Sebastian Brock (Crestwood, NY: SVS Press, 1990), p. 96.

garden'?" ² And the woman said to the serpent, "We may eat of the fruit of the garden trees, ³ but God said, 'You shall not eat of the fruit of the tree that is in the midst of the garden, neither shall you touch it, lest you die.'" ⁴ But the serpent said to the woman, "You will not surely die! ⁵ For God knows that when you eat of it your eyes will be opened, and you will be like gods, knowing good and evil." ⁶ So when the woman saw that the tree was good for food, and that it was pleasant to the eyes, and that the tree was to be desired to acquire prudence, she took of its fruit and ate, and she also gave some to her husband with her, and he ate. ⁷ Then the eyes of both were opened, and they knew that they were nude. And they sewed fig leaves together and made themselves aprons.

The narrator now introduces another character into his story with the words, **Now the serpent was more shrewd than any other living thing of the field that Yahweh God had made.** It is important in first interpreting this story to resist the temptation of importing lessons from a later Christian theology, forgetting we are still reading the literature of the ancient Near East. Questions of identifying Satan with the serpent will be examined later. For now we must read the story on its own terms. The serpent is present in the text not as God's evil cosmic adversary, but simply as one of **the living things of the field that Yahweh God had made.**

The serpent is described as **shrewd.** The Hebrew word used, *arum*, is somewhat ambiguous. It can describe the laudable condition of the virtuous and wise (thus its use in Prov. 13:16; 14:8, where the RSV translates it as "prudent"; Prov. 8:12 uses it to describe Lady Wisdom). It is also used with the more negative nuance of "crafty, wily" (thus its use in Job 5:12; 15:5, which says God frustrates the devices of the *arum*). The serpent was smart, but alarmingly so. Here it seems the word was chosen to counterbalance the naivety of the man and his wife. They were naked, vulnerable, arom, which left them open to the mischief of the serpent, who was *arum*.[17]

Serpents were often found in ancient Near Eastern literature and were associated with occult wisdom, health, fertility, magic, and divination.[18] They were also chaos creatures—liminal beings living on the edges, and thus forces against order. In the picture of death, chaos, and desolation in Isaiah 34:9f, the snake is classed with the hawks, porcupines, owls, ravens, jackals, ostriches, howling creatures, the hairy goat, and the night-monster. It is in this setting that the "snake will make its nest and lay *eggs* there, and it will hatch and gather them under its protection" (Is. 34:15, NASB). Not surprisingly, the greatest of the chaos-creatures, Leviathan, is described in Isaiah 27:1 as a serpent. Ancient readers of this story would have regarded the serpent not as definitively evil with a set evil agenda, but as an agent of chaos—as trouble, disruptive, a bringer of mischief.

The mischief and harm begin as the serpent says to the woman, **"Really! God actually said, 'You shall not eat of any tree in the garden'?"** The remark is not so much a question as a half-jeering exclamation, feigned surprise that God could have ordered anything so unreasonable. We note immediately several odd things about the remark.

First, the Deity is now referred to not as "Yahweh" (as in the preceding narrative) but, significantly, by the more universal and less personal appellation "God" (Heb. *Elohim*). This represents a deliberate step back from a person-to-person, name-to-name close relationship with God. By using this name the serpent already begins to separate the woman from her Lord.

---

17 Hence the choice here of rhyming English words: the man and his wife were *nude*, and the serpent was *shrewd*.

18 It is possible that the serpent (Heb. *nachash*) is here connected to the Hebrew verb "to practice divination," also *nachash*. If so, this connection would add to the threatening aspect of the serpent.

Secondly, the serpent deliberately misrepresents God's command.[19] God did not forbid the man and woman to eat from any tree of the garden. In fact He expressly said that they *could* eat from all the trees of the garden (Gen. 2:16)—all trees but one. By this misrepresentation of the command, the serpent begins his misrepresentation of God, portraying Him as unreasonable, churlish, and selfishly not looking out for the humans' best interests.

Most significantly in a Near Eastern culture, the serpent *addressed the woman when asking about both her and her husband* (in the serpent's words the "you" is plural). In our modern egalitarian culture this is unremarkable (and therefore rarely remarked on), but in Near Eastern culture, both ancient and modern, it is remarkable indeed.[20] A man would rarely address a respectable strange woman in public like this, especially in the presence of her husband. Queries would be addressed to the man. And in this story, not only is the woman addressed, but the serpent addresses his questions to her *when her husband is right there* (compare 3:6: "she gave to her husband *with her*"). For an ancient reader, this signaled that something was badly amiss and that more trouble was yet to come.

The woman's response was not encouraging. Far from yielding the lead to her husband, she took the lead and responded to the serpent's words, answering for both of them ("*we* may eat"), leaving her husband to stand mutely beside her. Her answer indicated that the serpent's insinuations had found fertile ground. She also referred to Yahweh as "God" and gave some indication that she found His single prohibition grating. God had forbidden eating from the tree, but she characterized His prohibition as including even touching

---

19   Note that the serpent cleverly did not call it God's "command"; his remark was not about what God "*commanded*" but what He "*said*."

20   Perhaps we may detect a cultural echo of this gender divide in the apostles' perplexity at Christ's conversation with a woman in John 4:27.

it. One can almost hear her frustration in being denied: "We can't even *touch* it!" It was clear that she chafed under the command.

It was in response to this expressed exasperation that the serpent moved from insinuation to contradiction, from remarking on how extraordinary was God's command to slandering His character. God had said, "in the day that you eat of it you will surely die" (Gen. 2:17), and the serpent flatly denies this: **"You will not surely die!"** Death is not so certain as that. God only said that because He **knows that when you eat of it your eyes will be opened, and you will be like gods,**[21] **knowing good and evil**. God is selfishly trying to keep you ignorant so that He can exploit you and is using the threat of death to cow you into senseless submission.

The half-truths are cleverly offered. It was true that if they ate they would know good and evil (Gen. 3:22); it was untrue that God wanted to keep this from them out of selfish exploitation of their innocence. Note that the serpent never tells her to eat. Having baited the hook, he simply stands back and lets his slanders do their work. He has implied, though without actually saying, that knowing good and evil—that is, possessing moral autonomy—will bring joy, growth, and fulfillment, all of which God is selfishly trying to keep from them. That, of course, is the trouble with half-truths; one always gets the wrong half.

The scene then shifts to the tree of the knowledge of good and evil itself. The serpent is not mentioned as being with her and her husband when she took the fruit, and there is no suggestion in the text that the conversation with the serpent occurred near the tree or even in the garden. Indeed, her reference to the tree as **the tree that is in the midst of the garden** indicates that the conversation took place some distance from the garden and the tree, for if she

---

21   Here *elohim* should probably be read as a plural, since the verb "knowing" is in the plural.

were at the tree then would she not have simply referred to the tree as "this tree"?

Her husband is still with her, as passive as before. (It is possible that he was not with her when the conversation with the serpent occurred but joined her later at the tree. But if that were so, his immediate and passive acquiescence in taking the fruit would not be narrated without comment. It is clear the narrator means us to understand his silent presence throughout.)

The case the serpent had made had worked upon her after the conversation concluded. It now seemed so logical: the tree was **good for food**, it was **pleasant to the eyes**, and was **desired to acquire prudence**.[22] It was thus nourishing, beautiful, and necessary for spiritual growth. The only sensible course was to reach out and take it. She therefore did so. She **took of its fruit and ate** it. After she had eaten it, **she also gave some to her husband with her, and he ate**. The man retained his passive role. She took the lead and provided food for him. No temptation was needed nor persuasion to force him to accept the forbidden fruit. She simply gave, and he obediently received and ate. The popular picture of naked Eve coyly tempting Adam by holding an apple owes nothing to the biblical account.[23]

The results were immediate and stunningly different from what the serpent had said. They anticipated that when they had eaten the fruit, their knowledge of good and evil would bring them joy. In fact it brought the opposite—the **eyes of both were opened, and they knew that they were nude**. The reference to **both** the woman and man emphasizes a shared plight. They had been led to

---

22 Hebrew *haskil*, from the root *sakal*, meaning "to be smart, circumspect, expert, skillful."

23 Especially in reference to the fruit being an apple. Some suggest the apple was chosen because of the similarity of the Latin word "apple" (*malum*) with the word "evil" (*malus*).

expect a common journey to joy and the heights of divine fulfillment. What they got was a common revelation of vulnerability and shame. Though the serpent was correct in saying they would know good and evil, he had lied nonetheless.

In a pathetic attempt to remedy the catastrophe, they **sewed fig leaves together and made themselves aprons** (choosing fig leaves because they are very large). The word rendered here as **aprons** is the Hebrew *chagoroth*; it is used in Isaiah 3:24 and 1 Kings 2:5 to describe a belt or sash, which gives the impression the leaves were not very adequate for the task. Before this, the man and woman lived together completely at ease; now they needed to hide from one another behind fig leaves. These were not the sublime heights of knowledge they had expected.

> [8] And they heard the sound of Yahweh God strolling in the garden in the cool of the day, and the man and his woman hid themselves from the presence of Yahweh God in the midst of the trees of the garden. [9] But Yahweh God called to the man and said to him, "Where are you?" [10] And he said, "I heard the sound of you in the garden, and I was afraid because I was nude, and I hid myself." [11] He said, "Who told you that you were nude? Have you eaten of the tree of which I commanded you not to eat?" [12] The man said, "The woman whom you gave to be with me, she gave me of the tree, and I ate." [13] Then Yahweh God said to the woman, "What is this that you have done?" The woman said, "The serpent deceived me, and I ate."

At length **they heard the sound of Yahweh God strolling in the garden in the cool of the day** (literally, in the "wind of the day," referring to the cool evening breezes). Note that although the serpent sought to distance them from Yahweh by referring to Him with the more generic term *Elohim*, here the narrator consistently returns to using the covenant and personal name for Him. It is their covenant Lord, Yahweh God, whom they hear **strolling in the garden.**

The fact that He called to them when He did not find them there suggests that each evening they would join Him in this stroll, taking fellowship together in the sacred garden shrine. Before this, the sound of Him would have brought them running in joy, like children to their father. But now, when **they heard the sound** of Him, they **hid themselves** from His presence **in the midst of the trees of the garden.** (The narrator refers to them as **the man and his woman**, in poignant reference to the original time of innocence when "the man and his woman were both nude and were not ashamed"; Gen. 2:25).

Not finding them as per usual, **Yahweh called to the man and said to him, "Where are you?"** Note that Yahweh assumed the man was the head and leader and addressed His question to him. Commentators have assumed that of course God knew where they were (since God knows everything) and that therefore all the questions He asked in this extended interrogation were feigned, asked to elicit not information but confession. That would be true if the story related history. But reading it as an ancient Near Eastern tale and as sacred mythology, one may take the story at face value, for the drama of the narrative is increased if the questions are real. God asked where the man was because He didn't find him at the usual spot.

The drama increases, and the tale is told with masterful artistry. The man and his wife emerge from the bushes shamefaced and downcast. The man answers, **"I heard the sound of you in the garden, and I was afraid because I was nude, and I hid myself."** One can almost see the man (with the woman a bit behind him, trying to hide?) standing there in his ridiculous fig-leaf apron, caught like a little boy.

The admission, however, revealed a further truth, one the man would have preferred not to disclose. But there was no hiding it. Upon hearing the man's declaration that he was nude, God knew that something terrible had happened and that the man had disobeyed Him. He therefore quickly demanded, **"Who told you that you were nude?** How could you know that unless you had disobeyed Me? **Have you eaten of the tree of which I commanded you not to eat?"** Note that God refers to the tree *not* as "the tree *of the knowledge of good and evil*" (as the serpent did), but as "the tree *of which I commanded you not to eat.*" The question contains its own blame.

The correct answer to the question was, of course, "Yes." (Or possibly, "Yes. I'm very sorry.") But the man does not so answer. Rather, he evades responsibility by answering, **"The woman whom You gave to be with me, she gave me of the tree, and I ate,"** as if this were all the woman's fault—and a bit God's fault, too, for giving him the woman in the first place. Once she was his joy, "bone of my bones and flesh of my flesh." Now she is "the woman whom You gave to be with me." The man sinned by passivity and failure to lead, by open disobedience, and now adds ingratitude to the list. His time with Yahweh God is not going well.

Upon learning that they ate of the tree, God turns next to the woman and asks, **"What is this that you have done?"** It is obviously not a request for information, for the man has just given this information. Nor is it so much an attempt to elicit confession and repentance. In its context it is more like a shocked cry of distress at the catastrophe they have brought upon themselves. The woman is more subdued in her response, but like her husband still offers no expression of repentance. She too does her best to shift the blame and simply says, **"The serpent deceived me, and I ate"**—three words in the Hebrew. One can imagine the downcast eyes, the muted tone, the heavy heart.

[14] Yahweh God said to the serpent,
"Because you have done this,
cursed are you above all animals
and above all living things of the field;
on your belly you shall go,
and dust you shall eat
all the days of your life.
[15] I will put enmity between you and the woman,
and between your seed and her seed;
he will strike at your head,
and you will strike at his heel."
[16] To the woman He said,
"I will greatly increase your pain and your childbearing;
in pain you will bear children.
Your desire will be for your husband,
and he will rule over you."
[17] And to the man He said,
"Because you have listened to the voice of your woman
and have eaten of the tree
of which I commanded you,
'You shall not eat of it,'
cursed is the ground because of you;
in pain you will eat of it all the days of your life;
[18] thorns and thistles it will bring forth for you;
and you will eat the plants of the field.
[19] By the sweat of your face
you shall eat bread
until you return to the ground,
for out of it you were taken;
for you are dust,
and to dust you will return."

Having heard all that He needed, God pronounced judgment, turning first to the serpent. Unlike the man and the woman, He did not need to interrogate the serpent to learn more of his part in this catastrophe. As a chaos creature, the serpent's role was clear and his fault obvious. God said to the serpent, **"Because you have done this, cursed are you above all animals."** The serpent might have been arum (shrewd), but he was now *arur* (cursed). Though one of the **living things** and **animals**, he was **cursed** and punished above them all.

The curse consisted of humiliation: **on your belly you shall go, and dust you shall eat all the days of your life**—you will go through life in lowliness, so abased and cast to the ground that you **shall eat** its **dust**. The sentence of being forced to go on its belly has led some commentators throughout the ages to surmise that originally the serpent had a different destiny. *Genesis Rabbah*, a Jewish midrash commentary on this passage, says, for example, "When the Holy One, blessed be He, said to the serpent, 'Upon your belly you shall go,' ministering angels descended and cut off his hands and feet and his cries resounded from one end of the world to the other' . . . Rabbi Issi and Rabbi Hoshaya in the name of Rabbi Hiyya the Elder said, 'The Holy One, blessed be He, said to the serpent, 'I made you that you should go upright like man, but you would not, hence upon your belly you shall go.'"[24] This interpretation regards the serpent, who was more shrewd than all other beasts, as having a greater destiny than the other beasts, but as forfeiting this destiny through its actions. Read as history or biology, this seems unlikely, but it is quite in keeping with a mythological reading of the story. A change is wrought in the serpent and in his destiny, even as a change is wrought in those of the man and the woman.

God further declares that He will **put enmity between** the

---

24   Genesis Rabbah, 20.5.

serpent and **the woman** and between the serpent's **seed and her seed**. There would be unremitting warfare against the serpent and its seed; the serpent's deed was doomed to have far-reaching consequences. (This is examined further at another place in this commentary.)

Next the Lord Yahweh turns to the woman. Though she took the lead in committing the sin (listening to the serpent and guiding her husband), yet she is not regarded by God as ultimately responsible. The man is the head, and thus he is ultimately responsible. Accordingly, God deals with the woman next, saving the man for the end as the one finally and ultimately culpable.

Though God pronounces the serpent cursed, no such curse is pronounced upon the woman. Rather, God sentences her to pain and weakness, saying, **"I will greatly increase your pain and childbearing"** (i.e., your birth pangs) so that **"in pain you will bear children. Your desire will be for your husband, and he will rule over you."** As the archetypical mother of the race, she would bear children, but what was originally to be accomplished with effortless joy will now be accomplished with **pain** (Heb. *etsev*). Moreover, in this new weakened state she will **desire** her **husband**, craving his protection, and **he will rule over you**. The word here for *rule* is not *radah* (the word used in Gen. 1:28 for mankind's subduing rule over creation), but rather *mashal*, the word used for the beneficent rule of the sun and moon over the day and night. The picture is one of the woman's weakness, in which she fulfills her task in pain and vulnerability, requiring the help and protection of her husband. She had functioned as his leader in rebellion against God but now was reduced to needing his protection against the world.

Finally God comes to the man, and He blames him because he **listened to the voice of** his **woman**. He should have been her leader, warning his beloved of the danger, correcting her, saving her from the deceiving words of the serpent. Instead he **listened** to her—obeyed her—and had **eaten of the** forbidden **tree**. Like his wife, he is not cursed either, but **the ground** which is his natural ecological partner is **cursed**. As the man (Heb. *adam*), he was taken from the ground (Heb. *adamah*) and was called to work with it, bringing from it the fruits of life. Just as his wife must still fulfill her feminine function of bearing children but must now fulfill that task with pain (Heb. *etsev*), so with the man as well. He must still fulfill his masculine function of working with the ground, but must now fulfill this task **in pain** (Heb. *etsev*), earning and **eating** his **bread** through labor, in **the sweat of** his **face**. This was to have been done effortlessly, the ground easily bringing forth its plants as when it once sprouted spontaneously for God (Gen. 2:9). Now the ground was cursed, and it would yield its fruit only with difficulty, bringing forth also **thorns and thistles**, as the man toiled hard over it. The man was sentenced to work the ground with ceaseless sweat, laboring over the ground until he finally returned to it himself, and death brought an end to his toil.

Though he along with his wife had aspired to become gods, in reality he was **dust**, like the ground over which he toiled. **Out of** this dust he once was taken, and **to** this **dust** he would one day **return**. God had said that if he ate from the prohibited tree he would surely die, and this sentence would find its fulfillment. One day he and his seed would die and return to the dust from which they once were taken. It is true that God did not plainly say "Now you will die" as a fulfillment of the threatened punishment. But the expulsion from the garden sentenced the man and his wife to a life of toil, pain, and frustration—that is, to dwell in the land of death, far from their home and from the tree of life. That was death indeed, as God had promised.

²⁰ The man called his woman's name "Life," because she was the mother of all living. ²¹ And Yahweh God made for the man and for his woman garments of skins and clothed them.

Before narrating how the divine sentence was carried out, the narrator inserts two words of hope. God told the man to give names to all, and he had previously cried out ecstatically that his newly discovered gift was *ishah*, woman. Now he more formally bestowed a name upon her and **called his woman's name "Life."**²⁵ In naming her, it seems he returned to his role as leader, which he had catastrophically abandoned. And yet by this name he honors her, exalting her as **the mother of all living**. That is, by this name he looked ahead to the future, to the time when they would together populate the world. Despite her role in the catastrophe, he did not abandon her or blame her. They still belonged to each other and together must make their way in the world under new and challenging circumstances. The name looked to the future with hope.

As well as a new name denoting a new role and future, we also find a new robe. **Yahweh God made for the man and his woman garments of skins and clothed them**. With its connection to the previous verse, this also represents a note of hope and grace. There was no going back, and they could no longer appear before Him naked as before. Garments were now required, even as the priests would later be required to appear before God sufficiently covered (Ex. 20:26). But the pathetic fig-leaf aprons would not do, and God made them more adequate garments of skins.

---

25 In Hebrew, she is called *Chawwah*, because she is the mother of all the *chay* (which words may or may not be related etymologically). The Septuagint retains the wordplay at the cost of changing her name: she was called *Zoe*, because she was the mother of all *zonton*. In a similar spirit one might offer the translation, "he called her Livia, because she was the mother of all the living," but that the Latin name "Livia" has no etymological connection with the word "living."

The word rendered here **garment** is the Hebrew *ketoneth*, the word also used in Genesis 37:3 to describe Joseph's "coat of many colors" and in Exodus 28:39 to describe the garment of the priests. There is no suggestion in the text that animal sacrifice was required to provide for the skins,[26] and had something as momentous as sacrifice then been instituted by God, it is inconceivable that the narrator would have let it pass without comment. The question, "Then where did they get the skins?" assumes an historical reading of the text. A more mythological approach allows the question to be sidestepped, as the narrator intended.

> [22] Then Yahweh God said, "Behold! the man has become like one of us in knowing good and evil. Now, lest he send out his hand and take also of the tree of life and eat and live forever—"
> [23] therefore Yahweh God sent him out from the garden of Eden to serve the ground from which he was taken. [24] He drove out the man, and at the east of the garden of Eden He stationed the cherubim and the flaming sword that whirled around to guard the way to the tree of life.

The narrator now resumes the account of the interrogation and punishment. Speaking to His heavenly council, **Yahweh God said, "Behold! the man[27] has become like one of us in knowing good and evil. Now, lest he send out his hand and take also of the tree of life and eat and live forever—"** The sentence remains unfinished, though its intent is clear. Such a breaking off in mid-sentence is rare in reporting the words of God. It is almost as if God acts with vigor and haste, taking action before He can finish the sentence.

---

26   One Jewish tradition suggests that the skin was the sloughed-off skin of the serpent.

27   Note the priority of the man: both the man and the woman had sinned, yet God refers to both of them under the heading of the *adam*.

It was God's prerogative to "know good and evil" and possess such sovereign moral autonomy. It was man's role to accept God's sovereignty and to be guided by God's decisions, not to snatch the right to be the captain of his own soul. Man had rebelliously reached out his hand to take from the forbidden tree. Now, **lest he send out his hand** again and **take also of the tree of life,** he must be expelled from the garden.

Commentators have sometimes suggested that this barring of man from the tree of life was in reality an act of divine kindness, saving man from an endless life of misery and fallen horror. That is a valid theological observation but not true exegesis. In the text, God had promised that if man ate from the forbidden tree he would surely die, and this refusal of access to the tree of life must be interpreted as the fulfillment of that promise—in other words, as a punishment, not a mercy. Man had been created mortal and subject to death, a creature of dust. The presence of the tree of life in the midst of the garden suggests that God had intended immortality for him if he had continued to obey. But now man had forfeited such a provision of immortality—he would be denied access to the tree of life and would return to the dust from which he was taken. God's threatened sentence would thus be carried out.

So God **sent him out from the garden of Eden.** The word rendered **sent out** is the same used in the previous sentence (there awkwardly rendered **send out his hand**), the Hebrew *shalach.* Its use here is intentional: lest the man send out his hand, God will send him out of the garden. Man's task on the outside will remain the same as before, for he must still **serve the ground from which he was taken,** tilling it to gather its fruit (compare Gen. 2:15). But on the outside, he will serve and till the ground in sorrow, far from God and the tree of life.

Consistently with His promise of punishment, therefore, God

drove out the man[28] from **the garden**. The Hebrew verb used here is a different one from the previous *shalach*; it is *garash*, a verb denoting a more intensive action. It is the verb used in Exodus 23:28 to describe the divine expulsion of the Canaanites from the Promised Land.

At the east of the garden God placed **the cherubim and the flaming sword that whirled around to guard the way to the tree of life**. Evidently entry to the garden was from the east, as was the case in temples of the ancient Near East (possibly to allow the rising sun to fall upon the image of the god set up in the western part of the temple). Entry to the tabernacle was also from the east. Accordingly, God **stationed the cherubim** at the entry to the garden, His throne guardians to bar the way, much as the Levites would later bar unauthorized entry to the tabernacle in the wilderness (Num. 1:51f). They were assisted by **the flaming sword that whirled around**. The image of the sword seems to be one of lightning, striking wherever one might seek illicit entry.

The way to the tree of life had been thoroughly lost, forfeited through sin. There was no going back. The former days of innocence, bliss, and the possibility of immortality in Paradise had been lost forever. With these mournful words, the narrator draws his story to a close. The bright dawn of Paradise was over. The long and arduous road through this age was about to begin.

The Protoevangelium

In Genesis 3:15, in his curse upon the serpent, God said He would put enmity between the serpent and the woman and between his seed and her seed. This latter would strike at the serpent's head, and the serpent would strike at his heel. What does this mean?

The first question regards the significance of the serpent. As

---

28   See previous note 52.

early as the Wisdom of Solomon (in about the first century before Christ), the serpent was identified with the devil: "God made man for incorruption and made him in the image of His own eternity, but through the devil's envy death entered the world" (Wisdom 2:23–24). This commonplace is reflected in Revelation 12:9, which speaks of "the great dragon," "that ancient serpent who is called the devil and Satan, the deceiver of the whole world." These represent applications of the sacred text, fruit of examining its *sensus plenior*, rather than historical exegesis. That is, these applications are not wrong, but we must begin further back.

The serpent is present in the text as a chaos creature, one from a place of non-order in the world who brought disorder into Paradise.[29] The serpent's "seed" or descendants are not *snakes* but *people*—those who choose disorder and who do evil. This is an important theme in Genesis, which will soon, in chapters 6–8, relate the story of how such evil brought the Flood upon the world. Beginning with the serpent, human history has been the story of the cosmic and eternal struggle of good against evil, of light against darkness. The serpent's seed (evil men) will strive against the woman's seed (good men), and the struggle will be unrelenting. The mutual incompatibility and hostility between good and evil has been established by God Himself as part of His curse on the serpent, His hostility to disorder and evil. The text here reveals that the struggle will result in victory for humanity over the serpent, and for good over evil, for though the serpent will strike at the person's heel, the woman's seed[30] will strike at his head, crushing him and bringing an end to evil.

Moving from the sacred mythology of the text to lived spiritual

---

29 Thus Walton, *The Lost World of Adam and Eve*, p. 128.
30 According to the Septuagint's understanding, a masculine seed, for it translates the ambiguous Hebrew pronoun with an unambiguous masculine Greek one. Some commentators see this as evidence that the translators of the Septuagint saw in this seed a prophecy of the Messiah.

experience and Christian theology, one may ask what force was responsible in this world for bringing such disorder. The answer, of course, is Satan. And what force was responsible for vanquishing Satan and restoring peace and order to the cosmos (Col. 1:20)? Christ. We may therefore accept this verse as a *protoevangelium*, a first preaching of the Gospel, if interpreted through the hindsight of application. God was not here prophesying or predicting Christ's coming but promising the final victory of good over evil and peace over chaos. We who live in the light of Christ's coming know how this final victory came about.

Adam and Eve: Issues of Historicity

This commentary contends that the early chapters of the Book of Genesis should be read in their cultural context, as ancient Near Eastern literature—namely mythologically. We resist the facile equation of "true" with "historically true according to the canons and standards of modern historical writing." We therefore receive the stories as their original readers would have received them, as archetypical stories about mankind. In Genesis 2, *adam* refers to the archetypical man (just as in the first chapter *adam* referred to mankind), and the creation of the *adam's ishah* refers to the creation of all women everywhere. This seems clear enough from their very names, for the tale is about someone called "Man" and his wife, "Life."

In this tale Man was made as the special handiwork of God, created to serve as His priest. God rested and resided in the world as in His cosmic temple, and Man lived close to God, tending His world in intimate fellowship with Him. Humanity was to tend the soil and bear children, living in the world and ruling it with loving care in God's Name. This would in time open up unimaginable future possibilities for joy, life, and immortality. But Man chose to rebel against God's sovereignty, to deify himself and set up his own moral autonomy apart from God. Such rebellious self-deification shattered his harmony with God and led to his inheriting the world as we now experience it—as a place of struggle with evil, a place of sorrow, pain, toil, and death. Man retained vestiges of his former nobility, but the path to endless possibilities had been closed.

That tale, told in mythological terms of dust, breath, gift, garden, serpent, and expulsion, is true of mankind generally and of each human being in particular. This latter application is reflected in the Orthodox hymns commemorating the expulsion from Paradise on the Sunday before Great Lent, for it identifies the *adam* with each one of us: "The Lord my Creator took me as dust from the earth and formed me into a living creature, breathing into me the breath of life." "In my wretchedness I have cast off the robe woven by God, disobeying Your divine command at the counsel of the enemy, and I am clothed now in fig leaves."[31] This story is the story of our race and of every person in it.

But, one may ask, what about what historically occurred? What about the actual origins of our race according to the findings of the various sciences? What about evolution? I, for one, am happy to cheerfully confess my ignorance about the details and also my general disinterest in them. And I would be happy if some of our anthropologists confessed at least a tiny touch of tentativeness in some of their conclusions as well. When one looks at an artist's rendition of one of our supposed pre-human ancestors, gazing into those soulful eyes, one would never imagine that one was actually looking at a piece of jawbone and a few teeth. One thinks of Chesterton's remarks on such theorists: "We speak of the patience of science, but in this department it would be truer to talk of the impatience of science. Owing to the difficulty [of paucity of

---

31 From the "Lord I call" verses for Great Vespers.

evidence] the theorist is in far too much of a hurry."[32]

That said, theories of the development of Man from a pre-human hominid ancestor form our modern way of understanding our biological origin, and I am not here concerned to dispute them. Accepting them at least for purposes of argument, I would like to offer a fairy tale of my own based on them, one possible scenario explaining our origins. One could label it as our modern myth. I cannot take much credit for it, for C. S. Lewis already described it in his *The Problem of Pain*.[33]

Once upon a time, there were many hominids upon the earth, animals who walked upright and had such advantages as opposable thumbs. One day, by God's decision and gift, a new consciousness was found in this race, permitting it to know itself as special, different in kind from the other animals and not just different in degree. This new consciousness allowed the homind to reflect, to philosophize, to transcend itself in love, to create such wonders as language, stories, art, tools, wheels, and fire, and to know God through His creation. The hominid passed along this knowledge to its offspring, and a new kind of race began, one which had before it untold possibilities as gifts from God.

Then the hominid race decided it would turn from God and find its destiny and endless possibilities without reference to Him. The harmony was shattered, its possibilities for future glory never to materialize. Instead of experiencing harmony, the new race began to fight among themselves in ways the other animals never did. Its new consciousness remained but was used for dark things, such as murder, crime, ambition, lust, greed.

---

32 G. K. Chesterton, "The Everlasting Man," from *Collected Works, Vol. 2* (San Francisco: Ignatius Press, 1986), p. 173.

33 C. S. Lewis, *The Problem of Pain* (New York: MacMillan Company, 1962), pp. 77f.

Conscious of itself in a way it had never been before, the hominid race was also conscious that death was a tragedy, and it experienced death as bitterness, loss, and as something fearful. For animals, death was not fearful but simply the closing of life's circle, its culmination. The animals regarded death as they regarded everything else, simply accepting it as natural. Man regarded death as fearful indeed, an intrusion and a tragedy, a denial of all that had gone before it, something that cried out for explanation. And for all of this, there was no hope of remedy.

I suggest that this myth is perhaps compatible with the findings of the anthropological theorists and also compatible with our Genesis stories. Issues of historicity and science have little to say to contradict the sacred text.

Aging the Wine of Truth: Adam within Scripture

Surveying the entire sweep of Scripture, as century succeeded century and the New Testament built upon the Old, we see the same themes reemerging and being put to ever richer use. In particular, the *adam* (the noun soon being used as a proper name) appeared as the first person on a genealogical list in Chronicles 1:1 and again later in St. Luke's genealogy of Jesus in Luke 3:23f, for which Luke used the material of 1 Chronicles.

Questions about historicity did not concern either the Chronicler or St. Luke, neither of whom had cause to question the Genesis story's historical accuracy. But strict historicity was never their primary purpose in writing, and we should not be disturbed at the thought that later writers did not recognize the mythological nature of the first stories. The Chronicler and St. Luke were not misled but simply led, for the author of Genesis was primarily concerned not to record history but to offer lessons about human nature and society—lessons the Chronicler and St. Luke learned very well.

Each of the biblical authors who wrote about Adam had his own particular purpose, theme, and theological agenda, and the figure of Adam served each one in a particular way. The original truth presented in the opening stories of Genesis thus became richer and more polyvalent as the centuries of scriptural reflection on it wore on. The tale of the *adam* in the garden aged like a fine wine.

In the Genesis story, the *adam* first appears as an archetype. In the tale's first telling, *adam* is a noun rather than a name, and in his creation from the dust, his discovery of the *ishah* as a true part of himself, and his transgression and expulsion from the garden temple of God, we see a mirror of our own human nature, condition, and all. The first tale of the *adam* tells us we are made of dust and live only by the breath and gift of God, and therefore should not rebel against His commands. It tells us that a wife is not mere chattel to her husband, something to be bought and traded like an animal (or divorced). She is the husband's other half, his fulfillment, his completion, and God's gift to him. It tells us that the husband's abandonment of the call to headship and his refusal to protect the woman lead to disaster in society, and it tells us that disobedience to God's Word leads to death.

In Genesis, this first tale was soon used not simply for teaching archetypical truths but also for teaching truths about the multiplication of the race. The *adam* then became Adam, an individual with a spouse and children. Archetype began to shade into genealogy and demography as the race began to grow. The *adam's* progeny continued to reproduce—and to repeat the primordial rebellion against God. By using the *adam* as the individual named Adam, the starting point for the race, the author of Genesis rooted the race in Adam's transgression and identified as the defining issue for humanity the question of whether or not it would rebel against God.

The Chronicler, writing later in about the fifth century BC, revisited the figure of Adam and made yet another use of the story. The author of Genesis was concerned to tell truths about the nature of Man and the nature of human society. But the author of 1–2 Chronicles was concerned to recount the history of the southern kingdom of Judah in such a way that the embattled little postexilic community could face the future with confidence. In the narrative of the southern kingdom's golden age, the figure of Adam served to anchor the little postexilic community within world history. By locating David and his descendants on the genealogical world map, the Chronicler declared the cosmic importance of that community.

For us moderns, genealogy is of little interest, for we do not define ourselves by our past history but by our present power. It was otherwise for the ancient Israelites. For them, a firm genealogy secured one's credentials and gave one confidence to face the future. For the Chronicler, the actual historicity of Adam as an individual was of marginal significance. Of greater importance was the fact that the figure of Adam served to anchor little Israel among the nations of the world.

With St. Luke's genealogy of Jesus, the Scripture revisited the person of Adam once again. Like the Chronicler upon whose account Luke depended, the crucial issue was not historicity. Rather, St. Luke's purpose in recounting Jesus' lineage was to declare that He belonged not just to the Jewish people but to all the world. St. Matthew wanted to stress the Jewishness of Jesus as the Messiah of Israel, and so he traced His line back to David and then to Abraham. St. Luke stressed the universality of Jesus as the Savior of all men, and that is why he traced His line back to Adam, whom Genesis and Chronicles recorded as the father of all mankind.

In surveying the progressive sweep of Scripture, we observe therefore that each of these biblical authors built upon the work of the previous one. The Book of Genesis presented Adam as the starting point of the human race. The Chronicler built on this and stressed that Adam was also the starting point of the people of Israel, thereby setting Israel in the center of the world's history and presenting it as the one nation that was crucial to God's purposes for the world. St. Luke built further on this, presenting Adam as the starting point for the lineage of Jesus, thereby declaring that Israel found its universal destiny through Him, the universal Savior. Thus the theme of Adam as the first man bore ever richer fruit throughout the ongoing scriptural narrative.

St. Paul and Adam

It remains to consider the teaching of St. Paul regarding the place of Adam in his presentation of the Christian Faith. This is found in three epistles.

1. In Romans 5:12, Paul writes, "As sin came into the world through one man, and death through sin, and so death spread to all men because all sinned . . ."

2. In 1 Corinthians 15:21–22, he writes, "As by a man came death, by a man has come also the resurrection of the dead. For as in Adam all die, so also in Christ shall all be made alive." A bit further on, in verse 45, he also writes, "Thus it is written, 'The first man Adam became a living being'; the last Adam [Christ] became a life-giving spirit."

3. In 1 Timothy 2:13–14, Paul writes, "Adam was formed first, then Eve; and Adam was not deceived, but the woman was deceived and became a transgressor." He also writes in 2 Corinthians 11:3, "I am afraid that as the serpent deceived Eve by his cunning, your thoughts will be led astray from a sincere and pure devotion to Christ."

We may also mention the genealogy found in Luke 3:23–38, which traces Jesus' ancestry back to "the son of Seth, the son of Adam, the son of God" (v. 38). The question is: Does faithfulness to this New Testament material obligate us to interpret the Genesis accounts not as myths like other ancient Near Eastern literature, but rather as historical occurrences? Do we have to postulate an historical Adam and Eve?

It must be admitted from the outset that Paul and the other Jewish and Christian writers of that time did interpret the Genesis stories as if Adam were as historically concrete as Abraham, Moses, and Ezra. That is because (1) there was nothing in the sciences of their day to suggest that the texts and genealogies need be understood any other way, and (2) their literary exposure to the pagan myths of their day did nothing to enhance their appreciation for mythic categories or help them find such categories in the Hebrew Scriptures. For the apostles, myths were pagan stories about gods breeding, fighting, and misbehaving (see Titus 1:14; 2 Pet. 1:16). But their literary limitations do not define our boundaries any more than their scientific limitations do. Doubtless the apostles accepted as scientific fact many things we would now reject, but this does not limit us in our reading of the sciences. In the same way we may appreciate the category of myth when archaeology puts into our hands treasures unknown to the first century.

The stories of the first man and woman ("Adam and Eve") do indeed read as if they were history, but then all stories do, including Christ's parables. The decision regarding their historicity must be based not on whether or not they read like history but on the recognition that they belong to a particular literary genre. The story of the Prodigal Son reads like history, too, but we do not regard it as historical because we know it was offered as a parable, not as an historical reminiscence. Now that we have at our literary disposal other myths from the ancient Near East (a resource not available in the first century), we can also recognize that the early chapters of Genesis were offered to the reader as myth.

These myths, as stated above, were archetypical and told truths about all men and women. Thus Paul and the other New Testament writers might legitimately draw conclusions from them about the nature of men and women. For example, the danger of being led astray from pure devotion to Christ by the deception of evil men is a lesson legitimately drawn from reading the story of Eve's deception by the serpent (as in 2 Cor. 11:3). The spiritual priority and headship of the man and the danger of allowing women to lead in the church is a lesson legitimately drawn from the story of Adam and Eve's creation and their deception by the serpent when Eve took the lead (as in 1 Tim. 2:13–14). Paul may have regarded these creation stories as historically factual, but the use he makes of them is not dependent on their historicity. As mythological archetypes they offer the same truths as if they were historically reliable.

Yet we must still consider Paul's comparison of Christ with Adam, for his basic teaching is that as death came through a single individual (Adam), so life also came from a single individual (Christ). Does this not require an historical Adam? I would argue that it does not. Paul's main point is that cosmic salvation comes through the individual known to history as Jesus of Nazareth, and that it is through His death and Resurrection that forgiveness and life are offered to all and that the cosmos finds healing.

In describing this centrality of Jesus, Paul makes use of the biblical story of Adam, citing Adam's role in bringing death to the human race as a parallel. His point, based on the literary parallel, is not negated if that literary parallel turns out to have no basis in history. For Paul's purpose in writing was not to pronounce on the historicity of Adam or his primordial act of sin, but to declare and emphasize the centrality of Christ. One may rephrase Paul's words in 1 Corinthians 15:22 thus: "In the same way as the story in Genesis related how all died in Adam, in the same way all now actually find life in Christ." The Genesis story, historical or not, sets up the parallel Paul can use in describing what Christ has done.

But surely something is lost if Paul, as well as teaching about the centrality of Christ, teaches that death entered the world through a single act of sin. Don't his words in Romans 5:12f about death coming into the world through sin lose something if death had nothing to do with human sin? Granted that his teaching about Christ is not dependent on the historicity of Adam, what about his teaching about death?

We must first consider what Paul means when he says that death entered the world through sin. What kind of death? Death as experienced by human beings, certainly. But what about the death of plants, trees, and other flora? Does Paul's assertion that death entered the world through sin mean that before human sin occurred, leaves didn't fall and plants didn't die? Or what about the death of animals? Must we interpret Paul as saying that before Adam's sin animals didn't die? That carnivores did not exist? That the teeth of the lion, clearly designed for eating meat, were only used to graze upon grass? Texts such as Isaiah 11:6–9 are not relevant, for those texts are clearly poetic, describing the peace God will send with the Kingdom. They were not intended to be understood as teaching zoology.

When the New Testament refers to death, therefore, it refers to death as *human beings* experience it; this does not encompass the death of animals. For the animals (as for leaves on a tree) death comes not as an intruder and an enemy, but as the completion and fulfillment of the cycle of life; not as a tragedy or something fearful, but as the closing of a circle. In this sense there was death in the world even before the first human sin, for plants and animals completed their appointed span and died as part of God's plan.

The New Testament does not refer to this ending of nonhuman life as "death."

When the New Testament decries death, it refers to human death, and human death is different from animal death, for it includes loss of the conscious psyche or soul as well as the dissolution of the body. Human beings were designed to know God; their higher level of consciousness and self-awareness, intended to lift them higher, means that death is experienced as tragedy, as the intolerable frustration of the purpose of their existence, as fear and bitterness. As those endowed with an ontological link with God (a "soul"), their consciousness survives the physical dissolution of the body and continues in the next life—what the Scriptures refer to as existence in Hades, Sheol, the land of the dead.

It is just this experience of death that came about as the result of sin. Let us take the example of our fairy tale, our secular myth of the hominid endowed with self-awareness and transcendent subjectivity. As long as a hominid lacked this self-awareness, he was not a Man but an animal, and death had no more significance for him than it had for the rest of the animals. But when the hominid became a Man, capable of knowing God (and of sinning), the situation changed.

According to the Genesis story, Adam died by being expelled from the garden and denied access to the tree of life. He did not forfeit an immortal existence, for he never possessed an immortal existence in the first place—only the possibility of gaining one through future access to the tree of life. The truth of this story applies to our myth of the newly humanized hominid as well—when the new Man, freshly endowed with the capacity to know God, chose to refuse that knowledge and turn away from His sovereignty, he lost the possibility of immortality.

Yet even then, death for this new Man was not the same as death for the animals. For the newly endowed Man was no longer an animal, and he now experienced death as loss, both through bitter fear in this life and through misery in the next. It is as Paul taught: death entered the world through sin. This remains true whether the Genesis tale is regarded strictly as supplying an archetype (teaching that our human experience of death is rooted in our corporate rejection of God) or as compatible with our secular hominid myth (positing an actual hominid experience). The human experience of death entered our life through sin.

CHAPTER 3

Multiplying and Sinning

Living Outside the Garden

THE NARRATOR PICKS UP HIS NARRATION and relates the story of the man and his wife after their expulsion from the garden, as they began to make their weary way in the world. The focus is on both multiplying and sinning, and accounts of procreation/ genealogical lists are interspersed among stories of murder, killing, celestial violation of the daughters of men, universal corruption, the sins of Noah and his sons, and the hubris of building a tower. It is significant that no happy stories of human heroism, nobility, and self-sacrifice are included. The overall message is clear: the history of human growth and expansion is also the history of sin. Man grows in artistic and technological prowess as cities and civilizations arise, but the glory of such achievements is overshadowed by the darkness of rebellion.

4 Now the man knew Life his wife, and she conceived and bore Cain, saying, "I have gotten a man with the help of Yahweh!" [2] And again, she bore his brother Abel. Now Abel was a shepherd of flocks and Cain a tiller of the ground. [3] Some days later Cain brought to Yahweh an offering of the fruit of the ground, [4] and Abel also brought of the firstborn of his flock and of their fat portions. And Yahweh had regard for Abel and his offering, [5] but for Cain and his offering He had no regard. So Cain was very angry, and his face

fell. ⁶Yahweh said to Cain, "Why are you angry, and why has your face fallen? ⁷If you do well, will you not be accepted? And if you do not do well, sin is lurking at the door. Its desire is for you, but you must rule over it."

Now **the man knew Life his wife**. (We render the Hebrew name *Chawwah* as **Life** rather than the traditional Eve, keeping the connection with its first use in Gen. 3:20.) The Hebrew verb for **knew** here refers to sexual intimacy. It denotes not just physical intercourse, but emotional and personal unity also, a non-exploitative consensual union.[1] Its use here witnesses to the matrimonial ideal, showing that sexuality was designed to be more than the mere satisfaction of appetite.

When the woman conceived and gave birth, she said, **"I have gotten a man with the help of Yahweh!"** The utterance was not a theological reflection but an ecstatic cry of joy. This cry contains a wordplay, for the word **gotten** (Heb. *qana*) sounds like the name **Cain** (Heb. *qayin*), even though there is no etymological link. Some have considered as odd the woman's use of the term **a man** (Heb. *ish*) to describe a newborn, for *ish* denotes not a baby but an adult. I suggest that the use of the term *ish* is related to the use of the narrator's name "Life" for the woman—the woman's name indicated that the race would find its origin in her, that she had a glorious destiny. The birth of the first baby meant that this destiny had begun with the help of God, that the first individual, the first *ish*, had now come into the world through procreation and that human history was beginning. The cry of joy was not just over the birth of the child but over a new beginning of the race.

In time **she bore his brother Abel**. The contrast between the

---

1   One would express a merely physical sexual contact by the phrase "he went in to her" (such as in Gen. 16:2) or "lay with her" (such as in Gen. 39:7).

two births is stark: for Abel's birth there is no cry of joy; it is mentioned almost in passing. The name **Abel** possibly means "puff, breath, vapor, vanity." If so, we may have here a foreshadowing of his future, which was indeed to prove ephemeral. The words of Psalm 144:4, "Man is like a breath, his days like a passing shadow," would find fulfillment in him. We also learn that **Abel was a shepherd of flocks and Cain a tiller of the ground**.

At length the two brothers brought their respective offerings. The word for **offering** is the Hebrew *minchah*, which denotes an offering of tribute and loyalty; it is used in Genesis 32:13 to describe Jacob's present to Esau. A *minchah* was often a grain offering, but could be anything—Jacob's *minchah* consisted of goats, rams, camels, cows, bulls, and donkeys. Each brother brought a present from his own resources. Since Cain was a tiller of the ground, he **brought an offering of the fruit of the ground**. Since Abel was a shepherd, he **brought of the firstborn of his flock and of their fat portions**.

As it turned out, Yahweh had regard for Abel and his offering, but for Cain and his offering He had no regard. How this lack of regard was shown is not stated. One old tradition suggests that God showed His regard by sending fire from heaven and consuming Abel's offering while leaving Cain's untouched. More likely the regard or lack of it was the conclusion drawn by the brothers from their future prosperity or lack of it. The ancients offered sacrifices to obtain the blessing of the deity, which was manifested in subsequent prosperity and health. If Abel prospered after offering the sacrifice and Cain did not, they would have drawn the conclusion that God had accepted the former's offering while rejecting the latter's. No heavenly fire would have been required. In whatever way the divine reaction became known to the brothers, once it was known **Cain was very angry, and his face fell** (i.e., he was depressed).

Many have asked the question, "What did Cain do wrong? What was wrong with his offering?" Some have suggested, on the basis of the text saying that Abel brought **the firstborn of his flock and of their fat portions** while Cain simply **brought an offering**, that Abel's offering was more generous than Cain's—that Cain's offering was merely nominal and he was being niggardly. This seems to read a lot into the text's silence, which has not a word to say about the deficient quality of Cain's offering. I suggest rather that the text is deliberately silent about the matter, leaving us in the place of Cain to wonder what the problem was and to question whether perhaps God was not being somewhat arbitrary. If this is so, one must conclude that there was nothing wrong with the offerings themselves, but that the problem lay in the hearts of the offerers—which is exactly the view of the New Testament (see Heb. 11:4).

We note that Cain did not complain to God but simply sulked, angry and depressed. God in compassion took the lead and came to Cain, saying, **"Why are you angry, and why has your face fallen?"** There was no mystery nor arbitrariness about His response: **"If you do well, will you not be accepted? And if you do not do well, sin is lurking at the door. Its desire is for you, but you must rule over it."** The image of **sin** as **lurking** is an interesting one. Some connect the verb rendered **lurking** (Heb. *rabats*) with the Akkadian *rabisum*, a demon that lurked in doorways to threaten those within. Whatever the cultural background, the sin of anger was clearly threatening Cain, and so in mercy God warns Cain that he must conquer and **rule over it**. The word for **rule** is the Hebrew *mashal*, the same word used in Genesis 1:16 to describe the sun's dominion over the day—an absolute sovereignty. The lurking demon is about to attack, and Cain is in danger—now is the time for him to take action!

⁸Cain said to Abel his brother, "Let us go into the field." And when they were in the field, Cain rose up against his brother Abel and slew him. ⁹Then Yahweh said to Cain, "Where is Abel your brother?" He said, "I do not know; am I my brother's keeper?" ⁰And Yahweh said, "What have you done! The voice of your brother's blood is crying to Me from the ground. ¹¹And now you are cursed from the ground, which has opened its mouth to receive your brother's blood from your hand. ¹²When you till the ground, it shall no longer yield to you its strength. You shall be a fugitive and a wanderer on the earth." ¹³Cain said to Yahweh, "My punishment is greater than I can bear! ¹⁴Behold! today You have driven me away from the ground, and from Your face I will be hidden, and I shall be a fugitive and a wanderer on the earth, and it will be that whoever finds me will slay me!" ¹⁵Then Yahweh said to him, "Not so! If anyone kills Cain, vengeance will be taken on him sevenfold." And Yahweh appointed a sign for Cain, lest any who found him should kill him. ¹⁶Then Cain went away from the face of Yahweh and dwelt in the land of wandering, east of Eden.

As it turned out, Cain was not to prove successful in his struggle against sin. **Cain said to Abel his brother, "Let us go into the field."**[2] Note that the text describes him not just as "Abel," but **Abel *his brother***, as if to heighten the magnitude of the crime. It was no stranger that Cain slew but his own blood. Cain's invitation to **go into the field** with him is not included merely as a narrative link to the next scene but to show that the act was premeditated. The murder did not take place because a quarrel escalated and got out of hand. There was no quarrel; Cain lured his brother to the place selected for the crime, a place apart from their parents, and then

---

2   Supplied from the Septuagint. The Hebrew reads only, "Cain said to Abel his brother…," omitting what he said.

slew him[3] there in cold blood. God's question to Cain, **"Where is Abel your brother?"** perhaps indicates that Cain buried him in the field as well.

Cain's response to the divine inquiry, **"I do not know; am I my brother's keeper?"** reveals the depth of his darkness. It was not only a lie (for he *did* know), but also showed tremendous impertinence, roughly implying that God's question was unreasonable. Since he was not his brother's guardian, how could he be expected to know where his brother was all the time? Such a surly response arose from a heart burdened not only with glowing anger and smarting envy but also with stifled guilt. However, God's question was not based on ignorance but on knowledge, and in demanding an account of Abel's location, God was striving to elicit a confession of guilt. God knew where Abel was, for **the voice** of his **blood** was silently **crying from the ground** to Him. His words **"What have you done"** were not a question but a cry of horror at the magnitude of the sin.

The sentence was immediate: Cain was **cursed from the ground** that **opened its mouth to receive** the **blood** of the slain. Cain tilled the ground, which in turn gave him his food, but he was now **cursed** (Heb. *arur*) from that ground since it had opened its mouth to receive Abel's blood. Being an unwilling participant in the crime, the soil was now stained and would no longer **yield its strength** to the murderer. The blood within the soil cried out to God for justice—Cain might labor all he liked, but no crops would be forthcoming for him.

Since Cain lived by tilling the ground, this sentence meant his banishment. He must now be **a fugitive and a wanderer on the earth,** leaving his home and surviving as best he could by hunting and gathering. The phrase **a fugitive and a wanderer** is alliterative in the original: Cain must be *na'* and *nad*. The cognate verbs are

---

3   Not merely "kill" (Heb. *ratsach*) but "slay, cut down, slaughter" (Heb. *harag*).

combined in Isaiah 24:20, where the earth "staggers like a drunken man" and "sways like a hut." The image here is of someone staggering unsteadily through the world.

Cain's response was still not one of penitence but one of protest. As he keenly felt that God's response to their offerings was unjustly arbitrary, so he now feels that His sentence is unjustly severe. Indeed, the **punishment is greater** than he **can bear!** For not only has God **driven** him **today away from the ground** (i.e., from his home) and cut him off from protection (**from** His **face**), forcing him into a life of wandering far off, but this means that he will be completely vulnerable to everyone. **Whoever finds** him **will slay** him without fear of consequences. Cain seems unconscious of the irony: he slew (*harag*) his brother, and now he protests that any stranger might be able to **slay** (*harag*) him too. This seems to be Cain's point: banishment should be punishment enough, but here banishment is augmented with subsequent death as well.

The situation envisioned here is from a later time. Cain himself did not fear retaliation from an avenger of blood—for who then could fulfill such a role? An avenger of blood was a near relative of the victim whose responsibility it was to track down the offender and administer justice by killing him. Abel's only near relatives were their parents, for according to the narrative, no one else yet existed. And it is unlikely that Cain referred to such a task being fulfilled in the years to come by people not yet born, for his words clearly reflected fear of a present danger. Rather, Cain's complaint was that there was no one now who could fulfil the role of an avenger of blood *for himself.* The sentence for his crime had separated him utterly from family. In the later culture of Israel, what kept a person relatively safe from attack from outsiders was the assurance that if one *was* attacked, one's family would fulfill the role of avenger of blood and take revenge on the offender and his tribe. Such an assurance of vengeance acted as a constraint on wanton attacks from outsiders. As a wandering fugitive with no family to back him up and avenge him, Cain was left with no such protection. Anyone could slay him at will with complete impunity.

God insists that this is **not so**. He Himself will fulfill the role of avenger of blood for Cain, and He assures him that **if anyone kills** him, **vengeance will be taken on him sevenfold** (i.e., fully and abundantly). Cain was indeed banished, but he had not forfeited the protection of God. In fulfillment of His promise, **Yahweh appointed a sign for Cain, lest any who found him should kill him.**

Much scholarly ink has been spilled on this sign.[4] The Authorized King James Version renders the phrase, "the Lord set a mark upon Cain," with the result that it was popularly considered that one could recognize a murderer by his face, because he "bore the mark of Cain." Obviously such a mark in this instance would have resulted not in Cain's protection but in his doom. The Hebrew here for **sign** is *oth*, the word used in Exodus 4:8; 10:2, and Psalm 78:43 to denote a miraculous event. Accordingly we may here interpret the appointing of a sign for Cain as God's promise that should Cain ever be threatened, He would manifest Himself in some way so as to convince the would-be assailants that Cain was under His protection. Despite his crime, God would serve as Cain's avenger of blood and provide this protection.

The sentence was promptly carried out. **Cain went away from the face of Yahweh** (i.e., he left the courtroom of God's presence) **and dwelt in the land of wandering** (Heb. *nod*). The term "the land of Nod" does not denote a territory named "Nod" or

---

4   Among the more interesting guesses regarding what Cain's mark might be is the rabbinic one in *Berakhot Rabbah* 22:12 that God gave a dog to Cain to accompany him and keep him safe.

"wandering," but simply that now Cain's homeland was one of exile and banishment. He who was to be *na'* and *nad* (v. 12) now dwelt in *nod*, his own place. The land is described as **east of Eden**—far away from their first Paradise and experience of God's presence.

> [17] Cain knew his wife, and she conceived and bore Enoch. And he built a city and called the name of the city after the name of his son, Enoch. [18] To Enoch was born Irad, and Irad fathered Mehujael, and Mehujael fathered Methushael, and Methushael fathered Lamech. [19] And Lamech took two wives. The name of the one was Adah and the name of the other Zillah. [20] Adah bore Jabal; he was the father of those who dwell in tents and have livestock. [21] His brother's name was Jubal; he was the father of all those who play the lyre and pipe. [22] Zillah also bore Tubal-cain; he was the forger of all instruments of bronze and iron. The sister of Tubal-cain was Naamah.
>
> [23] Lamech said to his wives:
> "Adah and Zillah, hear my voice;
> you wives of Lamech, listen to what I say:
> I have slain a man for wounding me,
> even a young man for striking me.
> [24] If Cain is avenged sevenfold,
> then Lamech is avenged seventy-sevenfold."

The narrative resumes with a domestic detail: **Cain knew his wife, and she conceived and bore Enoch**. (The age-old question, "Where did Cain get his wife?" will be examined later. Here we simply note that the existence of his wife is assumed.) Cain also **built a city**, which he named **after the name of his son, Enoch**. The word for **city** (Heb. *'ir*) does not necessarily mean a vast metropolis. Any walled settlement would be termed a city. Founding a city was not incompatible with Cain's life of wandering. His exile did not entail a life of perpetual homelessness, as if he could never remain in the same place, but simply banishment from his life of farming the soil at his home. The text portrays Cain as making a new life for himself with progeny and success. His naming the city after his son[5] reveals Cain's desire to look to the future and to build for his descendants a new start.

As if stressing the success of Cain's new life and new line, the narrator recounts his genealogy: **to Enoch was born Irad, and Irad fathered Mehujael, and Mehujael fathered Methushael, and Methushael fathered Lamech.** This last (the seventh generation from Adam in Cain's line) was a particularly important figure in human history as offered by the narrator, for the text dwells on him and his power at some length, unlike his predecessors, who do not merit more than passing mention of their names. The text mentions his two wives, his sons' great accomplishments, and his personal power.

Lamech's actions, including his polygamy, have received a lot of bad press from the commentators. Whether the narrator intends to portray the polygamy in a bad light can be doubted, for the later polygamy of Abraham and Jacob is mentioned without negative comment. Rather, the fact that **Lamech took two wives** is mentioned as a sign of his power, wealth, and importance. The women's names, **Adah** and **Zillah,** are given in verse 19, since they reappear in Lamech's boast a few verses later.

Between them they bore three sons and one daughter, and the sons were responsible for much of the culture of the ancient world. **Adah bore Jabal; he was the father of those who dwell in tents and have livestock**—that is, he established the practice of nomadic livestock domestication. His brother **Jubal** was **the father of all those who play the lyre and the pipe**—that is, he was the first

---

5   Assuming that he did name it after his son; some read the text to say that Enoch named the city after *his* son (i.e., after Irad).

musician using musical instruments. Their brother **Tubal-cain** (the child of Zillah) was **the forger of all instruments of bronze and iron**—that is, the founder of metallurgy.

We see here again how the sacred text democratizes and ascribes to the common man an exalted nobility. In the ancient world, men were created to feed and care for the gods and their temples; in Genesis, men were created to rule as God's image and representatives. In much of the ancient world, gifts such as agriculture, music, and metallurgy were gifts the gods gave to men; in Genesis they are the result of human invention and industry. That such gifts all came from the sons of one man shows his tremendous importance.

Lamech's power also is expressed in his boast, which he phrased as a song to his two wives. We see here the parallelism that characterizes all Hebrew poetry, such as the Psalms. The stich **Adah and Zillah, hear my voice** parallels the stich **you wives of Lamech, listen to what I say**. This parallelism means that we should interpret the **young man** as being the same person as the **man** mentioned just before, so that Lamech killed not two different people, but one. The word rendered here **young man** is the Hebrew *yeled*; it need not refer to a child or person of but a few years.[6] The term simply denotes a person young enough to be still strong, one who has not yet begun to decline. The word is used in 1 Kings 12:8 to describe the contemporaries of Rehoboam, who was then about forty years old (1 Kings 14:21).

It is not clear what provoked the retaliation between Lamech and the unnamed man (Heb. *ish*). Was it the settling of a formal quarrel, such as by a combat or duel? Whatever the particulars, Lamech boasts that an insulting blow was abundantly requited, and the original offender lies dead. Lamech's ancestor Cain was great and important enough to be **avenged sevenfold**, but Lamech himself

---

6   The New American Standard Bible, for example, translates *yeled* as "a boy."

was so great that he would be **avenged seventy-sevenfold**. In the
contest between Lamech and the young man, there is no hint in
the text that Lamech was to be blamed, or even that the man's
death was intentional. The song and event in its context (along with
mention of his two wives and brilliant children) served to stress
Lamech's social importance, not his sin. Preachers may legitimately
read into the text and use Lamech for their own homiletical purposes, but sound exegesis will not read from the text more than is
actually there. Lamech, coming seventh from Adam in Cain's line
(as Enoch came seventh from Adam in the line of Seth), is described
at length to demonstrate how Cain with his line had indeed prospered under the protection of God.

> [25] And Man knew his wife again, and she bore a son and called his
> name Seth, for she said, "God has appointed for me another seed
> instead of Abel, for Cain slew him." [26] To Seth also a son was born,
> and he called his name Enosh. At that time people began to call
> upon the name of Yahweh.

After describing the fate of Cain and his progeny, the narrator
returns once more to the story of Cain's brothers, saying **Man
knew his wife again**. Note the description of the father as **Man**
(Heb. *adam*); the generic noun for "man" now functions as a proper
name. Here we see a parallel to the beginning of this narrative in
4:1, where the man's wife was called "Life" (Heb. *chawwah*). Common nouns and proper names here coalesce, for the narrator is not
simply describing episodes in the lives of two individuals, but the
story of the human race. Mankind and Life combine to produce the
lines that will populate the world. This union now produced **a son**,
whom she called **Seth**. The name contains another wordplay, for the
name sounds like the verb *shith*, "to appoint," for the woman considered this child as the provision **God** had **appointed** to make up

for losing Abel in such a terrible way, the present joy now replacing the past sorrow.

And **to Seth also a son was born, and he called his name Enosh**. The proper name Enosh is also a Hebrew noun for "man."[7] It is possible that the narrator is focusing special attention on the line of Seth as the line of Man. That would explain why both the founding father and his grandson were called "man" and the intervening son called "Seth": this was the line "appointed" to carry forward the continuation of the human race through Noah.

The narrator concludes the account of Adam's descendants, both the line through Cain and the line through Seth, with the note that **at that time people began to call upon the name of Yahweh**. As well as the arts of agriculture, music, and technology, a public religious cult began at that time. The details of what this cult involved are less important to the narrator than the divine name it invoked, for by saying that the first men invoked **the name of Yahweh**, he declares that Yahweh, the God of the Hebrews, was once universally worshipped. The gods invoked by the pagans were all upstarts and idols. The Hebrew worship of Yahweh, the narrator contends, was the survival of the original religion of mankind.

This contention should not be read as history, of course, but as polemic. The issue is not when the actual title "Yahweh" was used by the Hebrews or by anyone else. The issue rather was the truth of Hebrew monotheism and the illegitimacy of pagan worship. "The gods of the peoples are worthless idols, but Yahweh made the heavens" (Ps. 96:5).

---

7   See for example Psalm 73:5, where the two words for "man" are used together: "[The rich] are not in trouble as are other men [*enosh*]; they are not stricken like other men [*adam*]."

Where Did Cain Get His Wife? Issues of Historicity

As we read the story of Cain, we find evidence that we have not yet moved fully into the realm of actual history. Certainly the stories of Cain and his descendants are not mythology like the chapters preceding them, but we still find ourselves in the realm of symbolism and quasi-history. The story of Cain tells the tale of two brothers, one of whom murders the other out of envy and hatred. This murder is projected back to the time of Man's beginning and made to serve as the first event of history. We can find signs, however, that it does not properly belong to the time of Man's beginning and that we therefore are not reading actual history as such. We note the following difficulties in taking the story as history.

Firstly, the story assumes the presence of a tribal society containing such social institutions as an avenger of blood. It was such an institution that acted to restrain people from killing those outside their group, for the killer feared retaliation from the victim's family. Cain cites the absence of such an avenger as a reason for his fear of wandering—which of course assumes the presence of others who would kill him if they found him vulnerable. Cain's fear presupposes a later developed societal situation.

Secondly, Cain established a city when he wandered from his home to make his way in the world. This also presupposes the existence of a sizable population who could live in a settlement built by Cain—again the situation of a much later time.

Thirdly (and famously) we find that Cain was already married at the time of his banishment. The text does not narrate Cain taking a wife, but simply assumes her existence and mentions that "Cain knew his wife and she conceived." The text said nothing about the first man and his wife having children other than Cain and Abel, so where did this woman come from? Her existence, problematic in terms of the narrative understood as history, is no problem if one considers the story to have been inserted back into the narrative flow from a later time.

Commentators have, of course, suggested that Cain's wife was indeed one of Adam's other children, so that Cain in effect married his sister. There could have been, these commentators suggest, a long period when Adam and Eve had other children who grew and multiplied over many years, and it was one of these whom Cain married. Cain's murder of Abel could have occurred much later, after perhaps several generations.

This attempt to preserve the historical nature of the text cannot be sustained. The text clearly says that when Adam's wife gave birth to Seth, she said that this offspring was the one God appointed to replace Abel, whom Cain slew (Gen. 4:25). It would have been an odd thing for her to say if in fact after Abel's birth there were many other children born over the years. Seth would then have hardly functioned in her mind as Abel's replacement. And Genesis 5:3 makes plain that after Cain and Abel came Seth, listed as the next offspring. Adam indeed had other sons and daughters—*after Seth* (Gen. 5:4). Since Seth was born *after Abel's murder* and since Adam's other offspring were born *after Seth was born*, Cain could not have found another of Adam's children to marry. Presumably he did not return from his wandering later to take one of them as his wife.

Finally, we note that Tubal-Cain is described as "the forger of all instruments of bronze and iron" (Gen. 4:22). In fact the Iron Age did not occur historically until 1200 BC, and Tubal-Cain could not have forged tools of iron at that early date. Here we see another historical anachronism and a sign that the story of Abel's murder is being projected backward from a later time in Israel's history.

But what does that mean? The story of Cain and Abel is not simply a fragment from another literary cycle, clumsily and incomprehensibly ending up where it doesn't belong. Rather, the story serves to make an important point. By beginning the story of the human race with this murder, the narrator skillfully shows that all of human history is the history of violence. There are glorious things in the human story too—agriculture, music, technology, religion—but notwithstanding this, the story takes place beneath the shadow of that primordial homicide. Violence is what has characterized humanity since we first left the paradisal garden of God's presence. Having betrayed God, we now constantly betray one another.

That is why the story relates not merely the murder of one person by another, but the murder of one person *by his own brother*. All men are brothers, and yet despite this fact that we all belong to the same human family, we rise up against our brother and slay him. Whether within a tribe (when we call the killing "crime") or between different tribes (when we call the killing "war"), we are a race that kills each other. The myths at the beginning of Genesis reveal our true identity as God's representatives and image, and the nature of the world as His temple. This symbolic quasi-historical story reveals our true debased state now that we have defected from God's love. Human history is the tale of culture and death.

5 This is the book of the generations of Man. When God created man, He made him in the likeness of God. ²Male and female He created them, and He blessed them and named them Man when they were created. ³When Man had lived 130 years, he fathered a son in his own likeness, after his image, and named him Seth. ⁴The days of Man after he fathered Seth were 800 years; and he had other sons and daughters. ⁵Thus all the days that Man lived were 930 years, and he died. ⁶When Seth had lived 105 years, he fathered Enosh. ⁷Seth lived after he fathered Enosh 807 years and had other sons and daughters. ⁸Thus all the days of Seth were 912

years, and he died. [9] When Enosh had lived 90 years, he fathered Kenan. [10] Enosh lived after he fathered Kenan 815 years and had other sons and daughters. [11] Thus all the days of Enosh were 905 years, and he died. [12] When Kenan had lived 70 years, he fathered Mahalalel. [13] Kenan lived after he fathered Mahalalel 840 years and had other sons and daughters. [14] Thus all the days of Kenan were 910 years, and he died. [15] When Mahalalel had lived 65 years, he fathered Jared. [16] Mahalalel lived after he fathered Jared 830 years and had other sons and daughters. [17] Thus all the days of Mahalalel were 895 years, and he died. [18] When Jared had lived 162 years, he fathered Enoch. [19] Jared lived after he fathered Enoch 800 years and had other sons and daughters. [20] Thus all the days of Jared were 962 years, and he died. [21] When Enoch had lived 65 years, he fathered Methuselah. [22] Enoch walked with God after he fathered Methuselah 300 years and had other sons and daughters. [23] Thus all the days of Enoch were 365 years. [24] Enoch walked with God, and he was not, for God took him. [25] When Methuselah had lived 187 years, he fathered Lamech. [26] Methuselah lived after he fathered Lamech 782 years and had other sons and daughters. [27] Thus all the days of Methuselah were 969 years, and he died. [28] When Lamech had lived 182 years, he fathered a son [29] and called his name Noah, saying, "Out of the ground that Yahweh has cursed, this one shall bring us rest from our work and from the painful toil of our hands." [30] Lamech lived after he fathered Noah 595 years and had other sons and daughters. [31] Thus all the days of Lamech were 777 years, and he died. [32] After Noah was 500 years old, Noah fathered Shem, Ham, and Japheth.

The next section contains a genealogy consisting of ten generations from the first *adam* to Noah. Most moderns have little interest in genealogy (at least in biblical ones) and tend to skip them when reading through the Bible. It was otherwise in the ancient world, where an unbroken genealogical line from the past promised a firm foundation for the future. A man without a genealogy was a man without a history and without proper credentials. It was like having amnesia. The Scriptures look to the future with confidence and so of course delight in genealogy.

The information contained here is described not just as "the generations" of Man, as in Genesis 2:4; 10:1; and others, but as *the book* **of the generations of Man**. The addition of the word **book** (Heb. *sepher*, "document") emphasizes the reliability and importance of the information. In an essentially oral world and culture, things also written down were considered important because they could be consulted in an archive.[8]

Once again the text takes us back to the first creation story, citing the creation of **Man** or Mankind as consisting of both **male and female** (Gen. 1:27).[9] The name **Man** (Heb. *adam*) was bestowed on the new pair by God Himself. The narrator stresses this divine bestowal of name, for it shows that Man was given function in the world and dignity directly from the hand of God. Man was created in God's likeness, sharing His authority in the world as His image and representative.

The text goes on to affirm that **when Man had lived 130 years, he fathered a son in his own likeness, after his image, and named him Seth**. The repetition of the words **likeness** and **image** here is deliberate, meant to show that the Man's authority as creation's steward was not unique to the first *adam*. His progeny shared that authority too, as the gift of stewardship passed to them. Though the Man **had other sons and daughters**, these are not listed, for the genealogy is concerned only with the first son of

---

8   See John Walton and D. Brent Sandy, *The Lost World of Scripture* (Downers Grove: IVP Academic, 2013), p. 21f.

9   The narrator here reverts to the divine designation used in the first creation story: God is Elohim, not Yahweh.

each generation. After that first son, the narrator recorded the time remaining in the life of each father; in the case of the first **Man**, it was **800 years**. After this, **he died**.

These words set the formula followed in all the subsequent generations (with the exception of Enoch). In these records and numbers, scholars have discovered some exegetical dilemmas.

The first dilemma involves the accuracy of the numbers, for the Masoretic Hebrew text differs from the Hebrew Samaritan Pentateuch, and both differ from the Greek Septuagint. In general one may say that the Greek tends to add to the numbers of the ages of the men when their first son was born (for example, both the Hebrew Masoretic and Samaritan Pentateuch give Adam's age as 130 when Seth was born; the Septuagint affirms Adam was 230), and so it allows for a longer time from Adam to the Flood. In the Masoretic reading, the Flood came 1656 years after Adam's creation; in the Samaritan reading, the Flood came 1307 years after creation; and in the Septuagint reading, it came 2262 years after creation. Clearly one (or all) of the readings contain errors. Most scholars regard the Septuagint as the least reliable—it not only looks as if it has altered the Hebrew texts, but according to the best copies of the Septuagint, Methusalah survived the Flood by fourteen years.[10] The question of which readings are the most authentic we leave here to one side as unanswerable and use the Masoretic as our provisional best guess.

Another exegetical dilemma involves the slow rate of aging and the long lives of these antediluvians. If our understanding of the mythological nature of the creation stories is correct, we have no reason to regard our earliest human ancestors as having any greater longevity than we do—certainly not to the point of living almost a

---

10   Gordon J. Wenham, Word Biblical Commentary, *Genesis 1–15* (Waco, Texas: Word Books, 1987), p. 130.

thousand years. What are we to make of these large numbers? Not surprisingly, scholars have expended much energy on this question, with no suggestion winning universal approval. Where so much scholarly puzzlement remains, we cannot pretend to resolve it here. Rather, we can only offer a few comments and tentative suggestions.

We cannot help but observe that the ancients did not use numbers as we do today. We use them with as much mathematical accuracy as we can, so that if a journalist reports that one thousand people attended a rally when in fact only a hundred attended it, we blame him for his inaccurate reporting. But the ancients could use numbers for their symbolic value and expand them to make a point.

We see such an example of a symbolic use of numbers in the Sumerian King List, which some date to about 2000 BC. It lists eight kings and the lengths of their respective reigns over certain cities, and the years of their reigns were very long indeed. The shortest reign was 18,600 years and the longest was 43,200 years, for a total reign of all the eight kings of 241,200 years. Obviously these numbers are symbolic, chosen to accentuate the power of the kings.

We observe too that the ancients all believed that the first men lived for a much longer time than anyone else. Perhaps the figures cited here were enlarged to reflect this belief, for if these ancient men were portrayed as living lives of seventy years or less, they would appear out of keeping and unworthy when compared with common ancient assumptions of antediluvian longevity. In examining the list, we see that if one divides by three the figure at which each person fathered his first son, and divides by ten the age of each person at his death, the figures mostly approximate what are now normal lifespans. I therefore tentatively suggest that the original author who consulted the document/*sepher* for these figures enlarged the numbers available to him as above to honor his ancient forebears, and this accounts for the huge numbers.

Finally, we note several details from the genealogy. Enoch's lifespan was considerably shorter than any of the others', since he died at the age of 365, compared to an average lifespan of 912 for the others. His brief span was not the result of God's judgment on his sin, for the narrator twice expressly says that Enoch **walked with God**—the same phrase used in Genesis 6:9 to describe Noah, who was a "righteous man, blameless in his generation." The phrase **walk *with* God** (and not simply "walk *before* God"; compare Gen. 17:1) seems to describe an intimate level of communion. Enoch had an extraordinary closeness to God.

But what was meant by the phrase **and he was not, for God took him**? Some have suggested that owing to the fact that the same verb is used here as in Ezekiel 24:16 and Jonah 4:3, the phrase **God took him** here means "God took him through death." But if this was the case, it is odd that the phrase **and he died**, repeated in the other nine instances, was omitted. The omission of this phrase strongly suggests that Enoch did not actually die.

In the *Gilgamesh Epic,* the gods took the hero Utnapishtim from the earth to enjoy immortality after his salvation from the Flood. The deity blessed him and his wife, touching their foreheads and saying, "In time past Utnapishtim was a mortal man; henceforth he and his wife shall live in the distance at the mouth of the rivers." The *Epic* refers to him as "Utnapishtim, whom the gods took after the deluge; and they set him to live in the land of Dilmun, in the garden of the sun; and to him alone of men they gave everlasting life."[11]

Such a cultural background might inform our reading of God taking Enoch from the earth. This finds some cultural confirmation in the fact that Enoch was the seventh generation from Adam,

---

11   N.K. Sandars, *The Epic of Gilgamesh: An English Version with an Introduction* (Baltimore: Penguin Books, 1962), pp. 113, 97.

an important generation. In the Sumerian King List, the seventh king enjoyed a special connection with the sun god and was initiated into occult mysteries. We therefore conclude that the consistent later tradition that Enoch did not actually die but was taken by God from the earth to enjoy a special reward (a tradition reflected in Sirach 44:16 and Heb. 11:5) finds confirmation in the original text of Genesis.

We also note that Methuselah differs somewhat from the others in the list. He was very old when he first fathered a son and lived the longest. It is possible that these figures are based on a tradition of someone who indeed lived a long time.

Finally, we note that Noah is special in this list. Not only are all three of his sons listed, but he was much older than the others when his first son was born. If the other figures on the list were subject to a threefold multiplication of their ages when their first sons were born, Noah may well have been subject to double that, with the original author multiplying that age by six. This enlarged age (500 when his first son was born) would witness to his importance in the ongoing narrative.

His importance is confirmed by a prophecy uttered by his father, Lamech: **"Out of the ground that Yahweh has cursed, this one shall bring us rest from our work and from the painful toil of our hands."** The word for **rest** is the Hebrew *nacham*, which resembles the name Noah (Heb. *Noach*), although most suggest there is no etymological link between the two words. The prophetic wish of Lamech found fulfillment in his son Noah, for after the Flood, God promised, "I will never again curse the ground because of man" (Gen. 8:21). After the Flood, the stability of seedtime and harvest would be assured. After Noah, earth's security and equilibrium would be guaranteed.

The Antediluvians: Issues of Historicity

This genealogy portrays an individual known as "Man" (Heb. *adam*) as the first man and his wife "Life" as the first woman. He is offered as the first figure in a genealogy of ten generations as constituting the first men of the human race. That there are ten generations may point to a certain stylization, for we read in Berossus, a Greek writer writing a history of Babylon in the third century BC, that there were ten generations before the Flood, and Genesis lists ten generations after the Flood from Noah's sons to Abraham. It looks therefore as if the listing of ten generations was an ancient literary commonplace more than actual history.

What then are we to make of the listing of *adam* as the first person in this genealogical list? The author of 1–2 Chronicles, writing after the Exile, seems to have regarded him as an individual no different from the others on the list, such as Kenan, Mahalalel, Jared, and Noah (1 Chr. 1:1–4), and his lead would be followed by later writers, such as St. Luke, who uses the Old Testament genealogies as the basis for his own. (Though even here, St. Luke's point was not the historicity of an individual Adam but the universality of Jesus. St. Matthew traced Jesus' ancestors back to Abraham to emphasize that He was the Messiah of Israel; St. Luke traced His ancestry back to Adam to emphasize that He was the Savior of all men.)

How are we to regard Adam? Granted that he along with his wife is presented as an archetype, must we regard him also as a single historical individual?

It seems to me that the Book of Genesis combines mythology and history, for the serpent in the garden and the tree of life are clearly mythological, while the stories of Abraham, Pharaoh, and the Patriarchs clearly purport to be historical. The flow of the Genesis narrative begins with mythology, symbol, and transmuted legend and then seamlessly slides into history. This is not surprising, for when the author wished to record the prehistorical realities of how the world began and how it took its present lamentable shape, what else could he do but use the prehistorical? In other words, mythology and symbol were the only teaching tools available to describe something as large and overwhelming as world origins.

As G. K. Chesterton once said, "Strictly speaking we know nothing about prehistoric man, for the simple reason that he was prehistoric. The history of prehistoric man is a very obvious contradiction in terms."[12] But what cannot be described historically can still be described mythologically and with the artistry of symbol and legend. Indeed, only by using a canvas as large as myth, symbol, and legend can one paint a story as vast and universal as the author of Genesis wished to paint for us.

I suggest therefore that the author used the language of myth in describing how the God of Israel made the world as His temple and mankind as His priests. He used the language of myth to describe the creation of man and woman (i.e., the foundation of the human race) and how sin against our Creator caused and continues to cause us to forfeit our access to immortal life. He chose a story of fratricide to introduce all human history, thus characterizing history as a continual fratricide. And he took a number of prominent ancient figures, combined them with his original creation stories of the *adam* and his children to make up the traditional ten generations, and presented this as the beginning of history.

The result is not a falsification of fact but a work of art. The earliest names of history (such as Kenan, Mahalalel, and Jared) fit seamlessly with the story of the first *adam*. The dual use of the word *adam*, which can function both as a common noun meaning "mankind" and also as a proper name, itself points the way and suggests how history and myth may fruitfully conjoin. The mythological

---

12   Chesterton, op. cit., p. 175.

element of the *adam* is necessary because the author relates the tale of our creation, a truth too big to be stuffed into the small suitcase of history. The historical element of names such as Kenan and the others is necessary because the author is describing the state of the actual world we live in. Neither myth nor history alone would serve such a high purpose; the author needed to use both.

CHAPTER 4

The Return of Chaos

Noah and the Flood

T HE STORY OF THE FLOOD begins with a connecting link. Chapter five contained a series of generations and births, and here in chapter six we have another series of births—births that result from the unnatural union of the sons of God and the daughters of men. The monstrosity of it all is offered as an example of the degeneration of the race and a cause of the coming Flood.

6 Now it happened when man began to multiply on the face of the ground and daughters were born to them, ² the sons of God saw that the daughters of man were good. And they took women for themselves, whomever they chose. ³ Then Yahweh said, "My spirit shall not remain in man forever, inasmuch as he is flesh: his days will be 120 years." ⁴ The Nephilim were on earth in those days— and even afterward—when the sons of God came in to the daughters of man who bore children to them. These were the heroes of old, men of renown.

It all began **when man began to multiply**. This multiplying took place **on the face of the ground** (the *adamah*, soil, not the *eretz*), the choice of word perhaps stressing the earthbound nature of the race. We are creatures that do not rise to heaven, where the sons of God live. Our place is a humble one, on the face of the soil from which we were taken. Though the previous stories focused on the births of sons (Lamech's one daughter is mentioned only in passing in Gen. 4:22), here the focus is on daughters. **The sons of God saw** these women, and thought them **good** (Heb. *tov*, here meaning "attractive") and **took** them **for themselves** as wives.

Who were these **sons of God** (Heb. *bene ha'elohim*)? Despite suggestions that they were aristocratic kings (reading *elohim* here as a superlative) or the godly line of Seth, it seems clear that they were angels. That is how the phrase "sons of God" is used in Job 1:6 (and how the Septuagint translated that phrase in Job). The *Book of Enoch* in 6:1–2 interpreted them as "the angels, the children of the heaven," and New Testament writers understood them in this way also (see 2 Pet. 2:4; Jude 6–7). Other interpretations arose mostly because commentators could not see how angels could impregnate women, and so they cast about for other ways of understanding the passage. But we must first read the passage as its ancient audience would have done, and stories of gods interbreeding with human beings were common in ancient mythologies. Gilgamesh, for example, is declared to be two-thirds divine and one-third man.[1] Our ancient audience would have questioned the *propriety* of the angels' actions, but not the *possibility*.

The narrator inserts this fragment of myth into his story to illustrate how far earth had gone astray. In Israel especially, harmony depended on everyone keeping within their proper boundaries. The culture had a horror of mixing, which found expression in forbidding the mixing of animals, crops, and even different kinds of cloth in the same garment (Lev. 19:19). The idea that the sons of God overstepped the boundaries and now were marrying and breeding with the daughters of men meant that all barriers had been thrown down. Note that this implied guilt for human society as well, for

---

1   *The Epic of Gilgamesh*, op. cit., p. 61.

the text speaks not of the angels raping the women or otherwise forcing them, but of taking women in marriage—presumably with their consent, or at least the consent of their fathers.[2] Every boundary had been breached, and moral chaos descended upon the world.

The narrator also cites the presence of **the Nephilim** on the earth as evidence of a world gone dangerously awry. The meaning of the term *Nephilim* is uncertain; the Septuagint translates it as "the giants," and the term here would have fed the Israelites' sense of alarm about the state of the world (compare Num. 13:33). The term probably does not identify **the Nephilim** with the offspring of the sons of God, **the heroes of old, men of renown**, since the Nephilim were said to be **on the earth in those days** *and even afterward*—and the offspring of the angels cannot be said to have survived the Flood. It was a horrific world—giants prowling about, angels and women breeding demigods, a world of inverted moral order.

We note here how appropriate was the choice of a flood as the method of judgment and destruction: God had once restrained the primeval chaos, separating the waters above from the waters below (Gen. 1:6), and as long as the waters above kept to their proper place above the earth, all was well. Now the sons of God above the earth were no longer keeping to their proper places but were descending to the earth and taking wives from among earth's daughters. How fitting therefore that the waters above should in response no longer keep to their proper places either, but likewise descend to the earth. That is just what happened (Gen. 7:11) as the primeval chaos of water returned to blot out the moral chaos of sin.

Yahweh pronounced sentence: **"My spirit shall not remain in man forever, inasmuch as he is flesh: his days will be 120 years."**

---

2   The verb for *took* (Heb. *laqach*) is the usual verb used for taking a wife; see Gen. 4:19; 11:29.

The translation of the Hebrew verb and the meaning of the sentence are uncertain and contested. God's spirit is His *ruach*, the creative breath and wind that once swept over the primeval chaos and gave life. When He removes His *ruach*, all perish (Ps. 104:29–30), and here God promises such a removal, for Man is but **flesh**—weak and sinful, offering no hope that his sinful rebellion will ever abate. The time is set, and after **120 years** the judgment will arrive.[3]

> [5] Yahweh saw that the evil of man was great on the earth, and that every formation of the thoughts of his heart was only evil all the day. [6] And Yahweh regretted that He had made man on the earth, and it pained Him to His heart. [7] So Yahweh said, "I will blot out man whom I have created from the face of the ground, man and animals and creeping things and birds of the heavens, for I regret that I have made them." [8] But Noah found favor in the eyes of Yahweh.

As God once looked upon the earth and saw that it was very good (Gen. 1:31), so now He **saw that the evil of man was great upon the earth**—indeed, **every formation of the thoughts of his heart was only evil all the day**. Wickedness was universal, ceaseless, and deeply ingrained. God therefore **regretted that He had made man on the earth**, for seeing their evil **pained Him to His heart**. Despite mankind's heartless and ungrateful rejection of His ways, God was not wrathful or angry, as might be expected. Rather, He was brokenhearted. Such tenderheartedness in the face of rejection would continue to characterize Yahweh in His dealings with His

---

3   Some take "Man" to refer to each individual man, and suggest that God here reduces the human lifespan to 120 years. But nothing in the subsequent narrative supports this, for Noah lived for another 350 years after the Flood, and later on men like Arpachshad lived for 438 years (Gen. 11:12–13). The "Man" here must refer to collective Mankind, and the figure to the time Mankind had left before the Flood.

chosen people in the generations to come (see Jer. 2:5f; Ezek. 33:11; Hosea 11:2f; Matt. 23:37).

We must not read God's regret as some modern theologians do and speak of God somehow experiencing time as men experience it, of His making mistakes and being subject to a learning curve. As Christians we still find some anthropopathism here, poetically ascribing emotions to God,[4] and affirm that the Creator stands outside of time. All that the sacred text means here is that God saw that the earth needed correction, and that in His love He grieved that it had come into such a condition.

But He would correct it and would **blot out man whom** He had **created—man** along with **animals and creeping things and birds of the heavens**. The list of created things (given in Gen. 1) is repeated here, for God would allow the original chaos to return and undo all the previous work of creation. The verb for **blot out** is the Hebrew *machah*, meaning "to erase by washing." It is the same word used in Exodus 32:32 and Numbers 5:23, where this blotting out involved using water to wash away the ink from the page. Its use here is perhaps deliberate, for God intended to use water to blot out mankind and wash away their sin from the earth. At the end of this solemn and terrible news, the narrator sounds a note of hope: **Noah found favor in the eyes of Yahweh**. Perhaps all was not lost.

[9] These are the generations of Noah. Noah was a righteous man, blameless in his generation. Noah walked with God. [10] And Noah had three sons, Shem, Ham, and Japheth. [11] Now the earth was ruined in God's sight, and the earth was filled with violence. [12] And God saw the earth, and behold! it was ruined, for all flesh had ruined their way on the earth. [13] And God said to Noah, "The

---

4   The Septuagint translator seems to have resisted suggesting God would experience regret, and translated the verse "God *considered* that He had made man on the earth."

end of all flesh has come before Me, for the earth is filled with violence through them. Behold! I will ruin them with the earth. [14] Make yourself an ark of squared lumber. Make rooms in the ark, and cover it inside and out with pitch. [15] This is how you are to make it: the length of the ark 300 cubits, its breadth 50 cubits, and its height 30 cubits. [16] Make a roof for the ark, and finish it to a cubit above, and set the door of the ark in its side. Make it with lower, second, and third decks. [17] For behold! I will bring a flood of waters upon the earth to ruin all flesh in which is the spirit of life from under heaven. Everything that is on the earth shall die. [18] But I will confirm My covenant with you, and you shall come into the ark, you, your sons, your wife, and your sons' wives with you. [19] And of every living thing of all flesh, you shall bring two of each into the ark to keep them alive with you. They shall be male and female. [20] Of the birds according to their kinds, and of the animals according to their kinds, of every creeping thing of the ground, according to its kind, two of each shall come in to you to keep them alive. [21] Also take with you every sort of food that is eaten and store it up. It shall be as food for you and for them." [22] Noah did this; he did all that God commanded him.

The text now refers once again to a family history, the *toldoth* or **generations of Noah,** for the story of the Flood is essentially his story. In a dramatically terse commendation (ten words in the original Hebrew) we learn why Noah found favor with God: he was **a righteous man, blameless in his generation,** one who **walked with God.** That is, as a **righteous man,** he stood upright, rejecting the crooked perversity that characterized his neighbors. He was also **blameless** (Heb. *tamim*). The word is used to denote an acceptable sacrifice—in Exodus 12:5 the "unblemished" lamb is *tamim*—and when used of men it denoted soundness, wholeness, integrity. Noah also **walked with God,** as did Enoch before him (Gen. 5:24), for his character was like that of His Maker, and they could walk together as companions. And as Enoch was taken by God and saved from death, so Noah was chosen by God and delivered from death in the Flood.

God took the initiative, informing His friend that **the end of all flesh had come before** Him—that is, that He had decided upon earth's destruction and was about to carry it out. We observe here the condescension of the Most High, for He confided in Noah as if he were His colleague. It would be the same in the case of Abraham, the Friend of God: "Shall I hide from Abraham what I am about to do?" (Gen. 18:17). Because **the earth was filled with violence through** men, God would judge them. As they **had ruined** (Heb. *shachath*) **their way on the earth** so God would **ruin** (*shachath*) **them with the earth.**

Noah's task was one of construction, the building of an **ark** or floating box (Heb. *teba*; the same word used to describe a coffin), and God gives him the details for building it before telling him why it must be built. This emphasizes the necessity of obedience: Noah was to obey first, unconditionally, trusting that there was a reason for his task before he was told the reason.

The ark was to be made **of squared lumber,**[5] of substantial construction, not the usual small boat of reeds or skins common in his day for navigating through marshes. There were to be **rooms** in the ark (Heb. *qinnim*, the usual word for "nests"), for they would be in it a long time. It was large: **300 cubits** long, **50 cubits** wide, and **30 cubits** tall. With a cubit being about 18 inches long, the resultant ark was about 450 feet long by 75 feet wide by 45 feet tall. With three decks, its total deck area was almost 96,000 square feet. The ark was also **finished to a cubit above** (possibly indicating a gap above the upper walls to let out the birds later?), with a **door in its**

---

5   Hebrew: "of *gopher* wood." What was meant by the Hebrew *gopher* is not known; we adopt the Septuagint rendering.

side. One thing lacking in the construction was a rudder, for Noah would not be directing the course of the great boat. It would float helplessly on the water. Noah was not to pilot the ship but simply to trust God.

After giving Noah the details of his task, God gave him the reason for it, introducing it by a dramatic **behold!** God was about to **bring a flood of waters upon the earth**, and **all flesh in which is the spirit** or breath **of life on the earth** would **die**. God stresses the universality and totality of the devastation by repeating the words **all flesh** and **everything**. Nothing would escape. Noah could not flee to safety; the only hope of survival was in the ark.

God promised to **confirm** His **covenant** with Noah. Note: not "make" a covenant, but **confirm** it, for as one who walked with God, Noah was already in covenant with Him. They had walked together as friends, and God promised that He would not abandon him now. His love for Noah included his family also, and they must accompany him into the ark—him, his **sons**, his **wife**,[6] and his **sons' wives**, for a total of eight persons.[7] The Scriptures stress the importance of the family as the basic social unit over and over again—thus Exodus 12:1f prescribes a lamb per household, and Joshua 2:12f provides for the salvation of Rahab as well as her family. God deals with us as parts of families, both in salvation and in judgment (compare Deut. 5:9, which speaks of God's punishment of the wicked "to the third and fourth generation"—i.e., all the generations living as part of the wicked household).

---

6   Noah's sons are consistently mentioned after Noah, and before Noah's wife or the sons' wives. The emphasis falls on the sons as the progenitors of the new race, rather than on the women or Noah's personal domestic situation.

7   The number is significant in the New Testament as the number of new life, of the eighth day, the day of eternity. Thus Peter stresses the number in his New Testament reflections of Noah's typological significance in 1 Peter 3:20f; 2 Peter 2:5.

THE RETURN OF CHAOS

As well as himself and his family, Noah must take animals into the ark by pairs, **two each, male and female**, to preserve animal life also, and of course to provide **food** for all to eat. Noah hearkened to all of this, but the sacred text records no reply; it simply says that he **did all that God commanded him**. Indeed, throughout all the narrative of the Flood, Noah never says anything. He is the silent servant. He never questions; he simply obeys.

7 Then Yahweh said to Noah, "Go into the ark, you and all your household, for I have seen that you are righteous before Me in this generation. ² Take with you seven pairs of all clean animals, the male and his mate, and a pair of the animals that are not clean, the male and his mate, ³ and seven pairs of the birds of the heavens also, male and female, to keep their seed alive on the face of all the earth. ⁴ For in seven days I will send rain on the earth forty days and forty nights, and every living thing that I have made I will blot out from the face of the ground." ⁵ And Noah did all that Yahweh had commanded him. ⁶ Noah was six hundred years old when the flood of waters came upon the earth. ⁷ And Noah and his sons and his wife and his sons' wives with him went into the ark to escape the waters of the flood. ⁸ Of clean animals, and of animals that are not clean, and of birds, and of everything that creeps on the ground, ⁹ two and two, male and female, went into the ark with Noah, as God had commanded Noah. ¹⁰ And after seven days the waters of the flood came upon the earth.

After Noah had done all that he was commanded and had built the ark, **Yahweh** then sent **into the ark Noah** and **all his household**, for as well as seeing that the world was wicked, He had also **seen** that Noah was **righteous** (his family being included since Noah could not be considered apart from his family). As a righteous Lord, He would never condemn the innocent with the guilty (Gen. 18:23). The time to save Noah had come.

We note throughout this story the alternation of the divine name Elohim (e.g., in 6:22) with Yahweh (e.g., in 7:1). Though they both form parts of the compound name Yahweh Elohim (e.g., in Gen. 2:4), in general the name *Elohim*/God is used here when the narrator describes God's relation to the universe, while the name Yahweh is used when describing a more intimate covenant relationship. But verses such as 7:16, which say that Noah's family "went into [the ark] as *Elohim* commanded him; and Yahweh shut him in," show that the alternating use of names might be simply stylistic.[8]

After Yahweh told Noah to enter the ark, He elaborated on His original order of taking animals into the ark by pairs and ordered Noah to **take** with him into the ark *seven* **pairs of all clean animals** (so that a clean acceptable sacrifice could be offered later; Gen. 8:20) and also **a pair of animals that** were **not clean** (and so could not be used for sacrifice), as well as **seven pairs of birds**, so that all these might **keep their seed** and offspring **alive on the face of the earth** after the Flood. This was necessary, for **in seven days** rain would come which would **blot out from the face of the ground** everything not safely in the ark. The downpour would begin **in seven days**, before which Noah must gather all the beasts of the earth into the ark.

The fulfillment of this order is mentioned without drama, almost in passing. Noah did not have to go out into the world to collect these animals. Rather God allowed them to come willingly to him (Gen. 6:20: they "shall come in to you"). We can imagine the spectacle as pairs of every sort of beast paraded through the earth, converged on the ark, and meekly entered therein. Noah here functioned as the new Adam, exercising benevolent lordship over the

---

8   We do not accept the view that the different names represent two different sources.

THE RETURN OF CHAOS

animals. It foreshadowed his work as the new Adam, as through his sons the world was repopulated and remade.

Once again Noah obeyed and **did all that Yahweh had commanded him.** With his family and all the animals, as God said, he entered the ark. The narrator mentions Noah's advanced age— he **was 600 years old when the flood of waters came upon the earth.** The point of mentioning the age was not to suggest how hard the task must have been for one so old but to emphasize his venerable dignity. The narrator stresses again that God's word to Noah was fulfilled: as He promised, **after seven days the waters of the flood came upon the earth.**

> [11] In the six-hundredth year of Noah's life, in the second month, on the seventeenth day of the month, on that day all the fountains of the great deep burst forth, and the windows of the heavens were opened. [12] And rain fell upon the earth forty days and forty nights. [13] On the very same day Noah and his sons, Shem and Ham and Japheth, and Noah's wife and the three wives of his sons with them entered the ark, [14] they and every living thing, according to its kind, and all the animals according to their kinds, and every creeping thing that creeps on the earth, according to its kind, and every bird, according to its kind, every winged creature. [15] They went into the ark with Noah, two and two of all flesh in which there was the spirit of life. [16] And those that entered, male and female of all flesh, went in as God had commanded him. And Yahweh shut him in.

The narrator records the actual date when the Flood began, namely, **in the six-hundredth year of Noah's life, in the second month,[9] on the seventeenth day of the month.** The date was not recorded simply for historical precision but to dignify Noah, for in ancient

---

9   We note in passing that an annual heavy rainfall usually began in the second month in the Middle East.

culture such precision of dates was ordinarily used only when recording the accomplishments of kings. It also heightens the dramatic tension.

The onset of the Flood is described as the return of the primordial chaos, as undoing the creation. At creation the primordial waters were divided by the solid expanse God placed between them, which allowed dry land to appear. In ancient cosmology, there were the primordial waters above the earth and also below. Here the two waters came together once more, obliterating the order God had made. The subterranean **fountains** below **of the great deep** (Heb. *tehom*, first mentioned in Gen. 1:2 as the waters of primeval chaos) **burst forth**, and **the windows of the heavens** above **were opened**. The waters thus converged, flooding the world from below and above, returning everything to its original chaotic state. This deluge continued for **forty days and forty nights**, until all the old sinful order was submerged in death.

The narrator mentions once more Noah, his family, and the animals, listing them at length. By saying that these entered the ark **on the very same day** as the rains fell, the narrator heightens their sense of escape. As a final note, the narrator relates that after they had all entered the ark, **Yahweh shut** them **in**. This detail is not accidental; in the pagan versions of the flood story, it was the builders of the ark (Utnapishtim and Atrahasis, respectively) who shut themselves in. The narrator declares that Yahweh was the true hero of the tale and the main protagonist. He, not Noah, was the true Savior of the human race.

[17] The flood continued forty days on the earth. The waters multiplied and bore up the ark, and it rose high above the earth. [18] The waters prevailed and multiplied greatly on the earth, and the ark floated on the face of the waters. [19] And the waters prevailed so mightily on the earth that all the high mountains under the whole heaven were

covered. [20] The waters prevailed above the mountains, covering them fifteen cubits deep. [21] And all flesh that moved on the earth expired, birds, animals, living things, all creeping things that creep on the earth, and every man. [22] Everything on the dry land in whose nostrils was the spirit of life died. [23] He blotted out every living thing that was on the face of the ground, man and animals and creeping things and birds of the heavens. They were blotted out from the earth. Only Noah was left and those who were with him in the ark. [24] And the waters prevailed on the earth 150 days.

The Flood is described in military terms as having **prevailed** as it **rose high** and conquered the earth. Indeed, so high did the waters rise that **all the high mountains under the whole heaven were covered**. The picture is one of complete triumph, as even the proud and high things of the earth were submerged in defeat. The water covered all the mountains to a depth of **fifteen cubits**— about 22 feet.

The narrative concentrates on the chaos and destruction outside the ark, with not a word to spare about how the passengers were faring within. Were they frightened? Confident? Despairing? Patient? The narrator completely ignores their experiences after relating that Yahweh shut the door behind them. Instead he focuses the story on God's mighty power, not Noah's faithful patience, for God was the true hero of the tale. Noah and his family survived the cosmic catastrophe only by God's gift. The story of the Flood remains His story.

As the waters raged and rose, and the ark floated upward above the mountaintops, **all flesh that moved on the earth expired**; everything **in whose nostrils was the spirit of life died**. The narrator uses the words **expire** and **die**, rather than the specific word "drowned," for this death did not come through a natural disaster, but as a judgment from the hand of God.

The narrator once again lists all that expired—the **birds, animals, living things, all creeping things,** along with **every man**—recounting the original list of what God created to emphasize that this creation had now been undone. **Only Noah was left and those who were with him in the ark.** In this brief observation we see the reward of righteousness. The wages of sin were death. Only the one who walked with God was saved along with his family. Counting the first forty days of the downpour, **the waters prevailed on the earth** for a total of **150 days.**[10]

8 But God remembered Noah and all the living things and all the animals that were with him in the ark. And God brought a *ruach* over the earth, and the waters subsided. [2] The fountains of the deep and the windows of the heavens were closed, the rain from the heavens was restrained, [3] and the waters receded from the earth continually. At the end of 150 days the waters had abated, [4] and in the seventh month, on the seventeenth day of the month, the ark came to rest on the mountains of Ararat. [5] And the waters continued to abate until the tenth month; in the tenth month, on the first day of the month, the tops of the mountains were seen.

[6] At the end of forty days, Noah opened the window of the ark that he had made [7] and sent out a raven. It went to and fro until the waters were dried up from the earth. [8] Then he sent out a dove from him, to see if the waters had subsided from the face of the ground. [9] But the dove found no rest for the sole of her foot, and she returned to him to the ark, for the waters were still on the face of the whole earth. So he sent out his hand and took her and brought her into the ark with him. [10] He waited another seven days, and again he sent out the dove out of the ark. [11] And the dove came

---

10 We understand this from the dates given: the Flood began on the seventeenth day of the second month (7:11) and the ark rested on the mountain on the seventeenth day of the seventh month (8:4)—i.e., after five months of thirty days each.

back to him in the evening, and behold! in her mouth was a freshly plucked olive leaf. So Noah knew that the waters had subsided from the earth. [12] Then he waited another seven days and sent out the dove, and she did not return to him anymore.

Then **God remembered Noah** and **all that were with him in the ark.** The verb for **remember** (Heb. *zakar*) denotes not a mental activity but a concrete action. When God "remembered" Rachel, for example, He took the action of granting her conception (Gen. 30:22); when Israel was "remembered" before God, they were saved from their enemies (Num. 10:9). Here God took action by bringing **a *ruach* over all the earth** so that **the waters subsided.** (The Hebrew word *ruach*, here meaning "wind," has been left untranslated so as to hearken back to the *ruach* that moved over the face of the primal waters in Gen. 1:2.) As God's own *ruach* once brought order to the water of chaos in the first creation, so it now brings order to the waters of chaos in this second recreation of the world.

With both the subterranean and the heavenly oceans now effectively closed off, **the waters** of the Flood **receded from the earth continually.** The day came when the ark **came to rest on the mountains of Ararat,** and the day was so joyfully received that its date was recorded like a royal exploit: it was **in the seventh month, on the seventeenth day of the month—at the end of 150 days** after the rains first fell. The **waters continued to abate** for about another three months, until **the tenth month, on the first day of the month.**

The phrase **the ark came to rest** contains another wordplay in the Hebrew, for the verb for **rest** (Heb. *nuwach*) sounds like the name "Noah" (Heb. *noach*). (Another wordplay is contained in v. 9: **the dove found no rest** [Heb. *manoach*] **for the sole of her foot.**) The location where the ark came to rest is not known; the

mountains of Ararat are a mountain range in the biblical land of
Urartu, by the east bank of the Euphrates near Lake Van.[11]

After another **forty days, Noah opened the window of the
ark** and **sent out a raven**. The **window** was evidently at the top of
the roof, open to the sky but not affording a view around the ark.
Therefore he needed help from the birds to learn of the condition of
the surrounding landscape, for opening the door on the side of the
ark would have spelled disaster if in fact the water had not subsided.
Sailors' use of birds for navigation was not uncommon. The **raven**
was chosen because it was a hardy bird, able to survive in the mountain heights, feeding on carrion. Though **it went to and fro**, it kept
returning, telling Noah that the waters were still present below.

Later Noah **sent out a dove to see if the waters had subsided**.
It too **returned to him to the ark,** and Noah **sent out his hand**,
reaching out to receive her, and **took her and brought her into
the ark with him**. Though one can see in this an image of tender-
hearted love for animals, the action was probably motivated largely
by a desire to learn more: by taking the dove in his hand like that,
Noah could see whether or not it had clay on its feet and thus learn
the condition of the ground. The test proved negative, for the dove
was not able to land, having **found no rest for the sole of her foot.**

Noah waited a week and then **again sent out the dove**, and when
the dove returned **in the evening** (the usual time for returning to
the nest), Noah saw to his surprise (expressed by **behold!**) that she
had **in her mouth an olive leaf**. The leaf was **freshly plucked**, not
flotsam floating upon the water. She could only have gotten that
from near to the ground, and so Noah then **knew that the waters
had subsided from the earth.** He waited another week and sent
her out again. This time **she did not return to him anymore** but

---

11   Mount Ararat in Armenia was only claimed as the location since the twelfth
century.

went to begin a new life in the restored earth. The time had come for Noah and his family to do the same.

> [13] In the six hundred and first year, in the first month, the first day of the month, the waters were dried from off the earth. And Noah removed the covering of the ark and looked, and behold! the face of the ground was dry. [14] In the second month, on the twenty-seventh day of the month, the earth had dried out. [15] Then God said to Noah, [16] "Go from the ark, you and your wife, and your sons and your sons' wives with you. [17] Bring out with you every living thing that is with you of all flesh—birds and animals and every creeping thing that creeps on the earth—that they may breed[12] on the earth and be fruitful and multiply on the earth." [18] So Noah went out, and his sons and his wife and his sons' wives with him. [19] Every beast, every creeping thing, and every bird, everything that moves on the earth, went out by clans from the ark. [20] Then Noah built an altar to Yahweh and took some of every clean animal and some of every clean bird and offered burnt offerings on the altar. [21] And when Yahweh smelled the restful smell, Yahweh said in His heart, "I will never again humble the ground because of man, for the formation of man's heart is evil from his youth. Neither will I ever again strike down every living thing as I have done. [22] For all the earth's days, seedtime and harvest, cold and heat, summer and winter, day and night will not cease."

Once again a precise date is given for such a momentous day. **In the six hundred and first year, in the first month, the first day of the month** (a wonderful New Year's Day), **the waters were dried from off the earth,** and so **Noah removed the covering of the ark** and looked out at the world. **Behold!**—to his delight, **the face**

---

12 The verb here denotes not simply "breeding," but breeding abundantly so that the world swarms with life.

of the ground was dry—that is, not covered with water. It would take almost another two months of waiting in the ark before **the earth had dried out** enough for them to emerge and begin farming. There are two separate words used here. In verse 13 the word *charab* is used, meaning "not wet". In verse 14 the word *yabesh* is used, meaning "completely dry"; its cognate is used in Genesis 1:10 to denote the land dry enough for man to live on.

We pause to note Noah's humble obedience. How hard and long those two months of waiting must have seemed! Yet he stayed within the ark until **God said to** him, **"Go from the ark, you and your wife, and your sons and your sons' wives with you,"** with all the animals gathered with them. We also note a subtle change in detail in this direction. In every other listing of Noah's family, his sons are mentioned before his wife (6:18; 7:7; 7:13), but here mention of Noah's wife precedes that of his sons—perhaps a sign that normal family life was being restored.

With joy all **went out from the ark**, and that **by clans**. This last word (Heb. *mishpachah*) indicates large extended groups of animals leaving together; the New English Bible renders it "clan" in Joshua 7:14—something smaller than a tribe, but larger than a family/household. It was a mighty and joyful exodus that left the ark!

Noah's first act in the new world was one of worship. He **built an altar to Yahweh and took some of every clean animal and some of every clean bird and offered burnt offerings**. These were offered as gratitude for their deliverance as well as to consecrate this new world to God. **Yahweh smelled the restful smell** (yet another wordplay; the word rendered here **restful** is *nichoach*, which recalls the name of Noah) and resolved **never again** to **humble the ground because of man**. Though the sacrifice is described as "restful" or "soothing," the idea is less that Yahweh was calmed and propitiated by the sacrifice than that He deemed the sacrifice acceptable. Noah's worship—and therefore the worship of the new world just washed clean from sin—would be acceptable and effective. We moderns take it for granted that God of course accepts all worship, but the ancients knew otherwise. Some offerings God would not accept (compare Prov. 21:27), but this offering was completely acceptable in His sight.

God and His world began again. The **formation of man's heart** was **evil from his youth**, and God accepted that this was so. If man *acted* on the evil thoughts of his heart, judgment would come of course, but the *presence* of such evil lurking within would be a fact of this new world. Accordingly, God decided to **never again humble the ground** (Heb. *adamah*) because of weak and fallen man. The word here rendered **humble** is the Hebrew *qalal* (not *arur*, "curse," as in Gen. 3:14, 17; 4:11). In this Flood God had humbled the earth, disdained it, cast it down into chaos and treated it with contempt. He would never again **strike down** the earth and its creatures like this. Chaos would never again engulf the ground.

Life could proceed on the soil in peace, for God and the earth were now at peace. The original blessings of creation were now secure: blessings of food, weather, and time, put in place once before, were forever assured **for all the earth's days. Seedtime and harvest** (i.e., food), **cold and heat, summer and winter** (i.e., weather), **day and night** (i.e., time) would **not cease.**

9 And God blessed Noah and his sons and said to them, "Be fruitful and multiply and fill the earth. ² The fear of you and the dread of you shall be upon every living thing of the earth and upon every bird of the heavens, upon everything that creeps on the ground and all the fish of the sea. Into your hand they are given. ³ Every moving thing that lives shall be food for you. And as I gave you the green plants, I give you everything. ⁴ But you shall not eat flesh with its life, that is, its blood. ⁵ And for your lifeblood I will

surely require a reckoning: from every living thing I will require it and from man. From every man's brother I will require a reckoning for the life of man.

⁶ Whoever sheds the blood of man,

by man shall his blood be shed,

for God made man in His own image.

⁷ And you, be fruitful and multiply, breed on the earth, and multiply in it."

⁸ Then God said to Noah and to his sons with him, ⁹ "Behold, I confirm my covenant with you and your seed after you, ¹⁰ and with every animate being that is with you, the birds, the animals, and every living thing of the earth with you, as many as came out of the ark; it is for every living thing of the earth. ¹¹ I confirm my covenant with you, that never again shall all flesh be cut off by the waters of the flood, and never again shall there be a flood to ruin the earth." ¹² And God said, "This is the sign of the covenant that I make between Me and you and every animate thing that is with you, for everlasting generations: ¹³ I have set my bow in the cloud, and it shall be a sign of the covenant between Me and the earth. ¹⁴ When I bring clouds over the earth and the bow is seen in the clouds, ¹⁵ I will remember My covenant that is between Me and you and every animate being of all flesh. And the waters will never again become a flood to ruin all flesh. ¹⁶ When the bow is in the clouds, I will see it and remember the everlasting covenant between God and every animate being of all flesh that is on the earth." ¹⁷ God said to Noah, "This is the sign of the covenant that I have confirmed between Me and all flesh that is on the earth."

Before God gave the earth into the hands of His new stewards, He bestowed a gift and **blessed Noah and his sons and said to them, "Be fruitful and multiply and fill the earth."** As the *adam* and his wife were first given the blessing of fertility and life (Gen. 1:28), so this second generation of stewards was given the same blessing. And to secure and protect mankind as they multiplied on the earth, God promised that the **fear** and **dread** of man would **be upon every living thing**—upon all the wild beasts, as well as on all that moved on the earth, air, and water. The primordial harmony between man and beast that existed at first had been shattered, and now dangers in the world from "nature red in tooth and claw" could harm man's growth. God provided here for man's protection by placing the dread of mankind over the animal kingdom.

Within this new and more dangerous world, God gave to man the possibility of hunting for food, saying, "**Every moving thing that lives shall be food for you**." Previously man's food consisted only of vegetation (Gen. 1:29), but now the eating of game was also allowed. God here made no distinction between clean and unclean food, as He would later for Israel in their food laws. Now seemingly all foods were deemed clean and allowed. But man must only eat of what **lives**—eating carrion and dead carcasses was not allowed by this provision. Before, only **the green plants** he farmed were his food; now **everything** was allowed. But even now, man could **not eat flesh with its life** (in Hebrew its *nephesh*, "soul"), **that is, its blood**. The blood must be drained away and not consumed as a foodstuff.

The point of the provision was not merely dietary but ethical. All life belonged ultimately to God and thus was sacred. This life was symbolized by the blood, and to claim ownership of the blood was to arrogate to oneself the sovereignty over life that belonged to God alone. God would therefore **surely require a reckoning** for taking the **lifeblood**, seeking out justice. He would require it from all, without distinction, **from every living thing** (i.e., every animal)[13]

---

13 This does not imply the moral responsibility of animals but that of their human owners. Thus if an ox gores a man and kills him, the ox's owner is responsible: if the ox was not known to gore, the owner would be penalized

and **from man**. God would hold **Man** (Heb. *adam*) responsible for the death of his **brother**, even as He held Cain responsible for the death of Abel.

Though life was cheap enough before the Flood, God now declared that life was valuable and sacred, for He **made man in His own image**. Murder must therefore be punished with death, other-wise the land would be polluted with the blood of the slain crying from the ground (Gen. 4:10; Num. 35:33; Deut. 19:10; 21:1f; Is. 24:5). God here mandated capital punishment for murder, plac-ing this responsibility for justice and the avoidance of blood-guilt squarely with man: **Whoever sheds the blood of man, by man shall his blood be shed**.[14] Because life was precious, the murderer could not avoid death himself simply by paying a fine, as in some ancient Near Eastern cultures. Blood demanded blood; otherwise the rich could literally get away with murder. The requirement is expressed here in poetry, showing its foundational importance to society (compare other such poetic utterances in Gen. 2:23; 3:14–19; 8:22). The society that refuses to avenge blood unjustly shed (including the lives of the unborn) lies guilty and polluted before God and subject to His judgment.

Given this preciousness of life, God repeated His blessing upon the race, bidding them once more to **be fruitful and multiply** and **breed**[15] **on the earth, and multiply in it**. Man could multiply in confidence that such multiplication would never again be nulli-fied by another flood. God emphasized to **Noah and his sons** (by

---

by losing his ox. But if the animal was known to be dangerous, the owner would be killed too (Ex. 21:28f). For the man killed by the ox was valuable to God; the owner of the ox cannot simply evade responsibility by saying that the ox did it, not him.

14   St. Paul would later confirm this moral obligation of society: the governing authority "does not bear the sword in vain; he is a servant of God to execute His wrath on the wrongdoer" (Rom. 13:4).

15   See note 81.

prefacing His word with **behold**) that He would never again **cut off all flesh** with **the waters of the flood**. This was His **covenant** and promise to Noah and his descendants, and to **every animate thing**, every living creature that had just emerged from the ark, whether **birds**, **animals** (i.e., cattle), or **living things** (i.e., wild animals). When He accepted Noah's sacrifice, God promised that He would never again ruin the ground with a flood (Gen. 8:21), and now He solemnly **confirmed** this by including it in the **covenant** He was making with Noah and all creation.

How could everyone know God would fulfill this promise? Because He gave them **a sign** of the **covenant** that He was making between Himself and **every animate being** (i.e., all living creatures; compare the use of the phrase in Gen. 1:20–21, 24, 30)—a **bow** set in the sky where all could see it.

The word for **bow** (Heb. *qesheth*) is the usual word for the weapon that shoots arrows (e.g., 2 Kin. 9:24), and God is portrayed poetically as shooting such arrows at His foes (Ps. 18:14). Here God declared that He would put aside His weapon and no longer treat the earth as His adversary, **setting** His **bow in the clouds** as a sign of the covenant for all to see. That is, the rainbow, visible even before this after it rained, would now serve as the universal promise that rain would no longer be used as God's weapon of destruction. When God saw the bow there **in the clouds**, pointing not downward to the earth but away from it, He would **remember** His **covenant** and not judge the earth as He had before.

God here spoke entirely for our sake. God did not require a sign to remind Him of His promise, but He spoke as if the rainbow served as His permanent reminder that we might be comforted and consoled. The rainbow thus reminds *us* of His mercy and covenant, not Him. We need not look up in fear each time the rains begin as if the beginning of the downpour might signal another deluge.

[18] The sons of Noah who went out from the ark were Shem, Ham, and Japheth. (Ham was the father of Canaan.) [19] These three were the sons of Noah, and from these the whole earth was overspread. [20] Noah, a man of the ground, began to plant a vineyard. [21] He drank of the wine and became drunk and lay uncovered in the midst of his tent. [22] And Ham, the father of Canaan, saw the nakedness of his father and told his two brothers outside. [23] Then Shem and Japheth took a garment, laid it on both their shoulders, and walked backward and covered the nakedness of their father. Their faces were turned backward, and they did not see their father's nakedness. [24] When Noah awoke from his wine and knew what his youngest son had done to him, [25] he said,
"Cursed be Canaan;
a slave of slaves shall he be to his brothers."
[26] He also said,
"Blessed be Yahweh, the God of Shem;
and let Canaan be his slave.
[27] May God enlarge Japheth,
and let him dwell in the tents of Shem,
and let Canaan be his slave."
[28] After the flood Noah lived 350 years. [29] All the days of Noah were 950 years, and he died.

The story of Noah ends with a connecting link to the next section. In chapter five the narrator records a table of the nations and of their dispersal and distribution over the earth. Here he narrates the story of the sin of one of his sons and how it brought a curse which would affect how his descendants would relate to one another as they dispersed and interacted. The story of Noah's nakedness and Ham's sin is thus not a trivial and meaningless epilogue to the story of Noah, a depressing denouement to the previous saga. Rather, it functions as a prophecy and foreshadowing of how Noah's descendants would relate to each other in the distant future.

The narrator sets the stage by repeating that **the sons of Noah who went out from the ark were Shem, Ham, and Japheth**. (Ham was the youngest, as we learn in v. 24; he is probably paired with Shem because the two names are monosyllabic and this listing of three sounds more euphonious.) In order to make sense of the coming story, the narrator adds that **Ham was the father of Canaan**. He also stresses that **from these three sons of Noah** alone **the whole earth was overspread** and peopled. They thus had a foundational importance for all that was to come.

The story itself begins by saying that **Noah** was **a man of the ground** (of the adamah, soil—i.e., a farmer), and that as such he planted **a vineyard**. The description of him as a **man of the adamah** links him with the prophetic hope of his father Lamech, who said at his birth, "Out of the adamah that Yahweh has cursed, this one shall bring us rest" (Gen. 5:29). It calls attention to the fulfillment of that hope, for Noah did indeed live to see Yahweh promise to never again curse the adamah (Gen. 8:21). His farming the soil, the adamah, celebrated the realization of that hope.

At length, after the soil had been planted and grapes harvested and made into wine, Noah **drank of the wine and became drunk and lay uncovered in the midst of his tent**. (The specification of Noah being **in the midst of his tent** is meant to stress that he was not drunk in public, but in private.) Certain groups have detected at least a hint of rebuke in the detail that Noah got drunk and have contrasted it with his previous commendation as being righteous and blameless (Gen. 6:9), wondering how could this be.

It is doubtful if the narrator intends much censure in his report of Noah's inebriation. References to a lot of drinking in Genesis 43:34; Judges 9:13; Psalm 104:15; and John 2:10 contain no hint that feeling merry with drink was considered reprehensible. Indeed, some stories of the ancient Near East portray some of the gods as getting drunk.[16] Public drunkenness was indeed rebuked in Israelite wisdom literature (e.g., Prov. 23:31–35), but it would be a mistake to read that rebuke into our present passage. The drunkenness is mentioned only because it occasioned Noah being privately naked in the midst of his tent.

Ham (once again described as **the father of Canaan** to prepare the reader for the coming rebuke) **saw the nakedness of his father and told his two brothers outside**. Modern readers are perplexed at what could be sinful in this—at least sinful enough to warrant such a stunning curse from Noah when he discovered it. Admittedly this "seeing" denoted intently gazing upon the father and not simply a quick and accidental glance. But even so, what was so wrong with that? Some suggest therefore that the phrase **saw the nakedness of his father** must refer to something more than a simple look—perhaps that Ham had sex with his father (or with his mother, given that "to uncover your father's nakedness" in Lev. 20:11 denoted having sex with his wife), or even that he castrated him. But the meaning of "to see his father's nakedness" must be determined by the reaction of Ham's brothers, **Shem and Japheth,** who acted so that **they did not see their father's nakedness**—that is, they **walked backward** into his tent and **covered** him with a **garment**. Covering his naked body with a garment without seeing him undid Ham's act. "Seeing his father's nakedness" simply meant gazing long at Noah's naked body, and then going outside to tell his brothers—doubtless to invite them to come inside and see his shame for themselves.

16   For example, a hymn to the supreme god El portrays him at a banquet thus: "El drinks wine to satiety, liquor to drunkenness. El goes to his house, Tkmn and Shnm [other gods] carry him out." Another Near Eastern legend says that a model son is expected to carry his father home when the latter is too drunk to walk. (Quoted in Hamilton, Victor P., New International Commentary on the Old Testament, *Genesis 1–17* [Grand Rapids, MI: Wm. B. Eerdmans Publishing, 1990], p. 321.)

In the culture of that time, such disrespect for the patriarch of the family was indeed unheard of and terrible, constituting as it did almost a rejection of his moral authority. Noah was in his private tent, and the act of entering and acting as Ham did constituted a tremendous boundary violation. (We recall that the narrator stressed how Noah was "in the midst of his tent.") Not surprisingly, when Noah learned of the outrage in the morning, he was incensed.

His response was to utter a curse, which in that culture involved not simply reviling or swearing at Ham, but invoking future misfortune upon him. Solemn curses were feared in ancient times and considered as possessing their own potency, to the point where Proverbs 26:2 had to offer assurance that a curse that was undeserved would do no harm. Noah's curse on the guilty therefore was a fearsome thing and could be expected to be potent.

Some perplexity has attached to the identity of the recipient of the curse, for Noah lashed out saying, **"Cursed[17] be Canaan"** even though it was Ham who actually was the offender. Canaan was to be **a slave of slaves to his brothers** (i.e., the lowest of slaves, in a place of total humiliation). Upon those brothers, Shem and Japheth, Noah heaped praise: **"Blessed be Yahweh, the God of Shem; and let Canaan be his slave. May God enlarge Japheth, and let him dwell in the tents of Shem, and let Canaan be his slave."** What did this mean?

We first note that the entire utterance concerns future generations (thus the reference to **Japheth** dwelling **in the tents of Shem**—i.e., the *descendants* of Japheth dwelling in tents of the *descendants* of Shem). The curse therefore was not uttered as a personal imprecation (such as "may misfortune dog you personally; may you sicken and die") but against future descendants. That also explains why

---

17   Hebrew *arur*, the same word used before to curse the serpent, the ground, and Cain.

Noah directed his curse at Canaan, for Canaan represented Ham's future line. Ham was the offender, and so the imprecation was against him—that is, against the destiny of his progeny.

In our radically individualized culture, we consider persons atomistically, regarding each person as completely separate from others. Thus a curse directed toward a father's child, for example, would be directed at *the child*, not *the father*. It was otherwise in the ancient world, so that an ancient reading of this curse would have understood it as directed at Ham *through his descendants*. In these two utterances, Noah established his will for all Ham's descendants, who would one day overspread the whole earth. That is, Ham's descendants through Canaan would be in perpetual difficulty and servitude (the reference to slavery is repeated three times, as Canaan would be the slave of the descendants of both Shem and Japheth). Ham doubtless hoped to enjoy a glorious future through his descendants; Noah effectively dashed that hope to pieces.

We note also that Noah, in blessing **Shem**, did not simply declare "blessed be Shem" (as might be expected), but rather **"Blessed be Yahweh."** Noah, learning of Shem's righteousness, blessed God in an ecstatic cry of gratitude. But the fact that Yahweh is described as "the God of Shem" meant that Shem could himself expect special protection and blessing from Yahweh, since Yahweh was his god in this definitive way. In this way Noah did indeed bless Shem.

In blessing **Japheth**, Noah not only subjects Ham's descendants through Canaan to Japheth's descendants, but also prays that God will **enlarge** him (with a play on words, for the Hebrew verb rendered **enlarge** is *yaphat*, which sounds like the name Japheth). The petition asking that Japheth's descendants would **dwell in the tents** of the descendants **of Shem** has occasioned some perplexity, as commentators try to identify which descendants could be meant.

Perhaps it is best to take the petition generally as meaning that Shem and Japheth may form alliances, but that Ham's descendants through Canaan will always be excluded. Fraternal unity will never be regained.

The fulfillment of this curse and these blessings will be found in their descendants. As the next chapter will reveal, Shem's descendants will be found in the Semites, such as the people of Israel. Ham's descendants will be found in the Egyptians (compare Ps. 78:51; 105:23; 106:22, which speak of Egypt as the tents and the land of Ham). Japheth's descendants include the Philistines and sea peoples, as well as those in Greece and Anatolia. Canaan's descendants, of course, are the Canaanites, the original pagan inhabitants of the Holy Land whom Israel displaced. The servitude of Canaan to Shem and Japheth would find fulfillment in the Philistine ascendancy on the Palestinian coast and the Israelite ascendancy in Palestine, in their own sphere, at the cost of the original Canaanite populations there. Thus, before the narrator lists the various nations that will overspread the earth, he gives us a prophetic forecast of their fate.

He ends this connecting link by placing the entire story of Noah and the Flood's aftermath within the context of the previous genealogy of chapter five. Consistent with the pattern found there, he concludes, **After the flood Noah lived 350 years. All the days of Noah were 950 years, and he died**. We find this pattern in Genesis 5:6–8, for example, with the exception that Noah's lifespan is defined not by how long he lived after the birth of his first son, but rather how long he lived **after the flood**. It was his role in the Flood that defined his life and was its crowning hour of glory, not the birth of his firstborn son.

The Search for Noah's Flood: Issues of Historicity

Many Christians are eagerly involved in the timeless "search for Noah's ark," which venture presupposes the historicity of the Genesis narrative. The whole topic has been enriched (or perhaps complicated) by the discovery of material from the ancient Near East that also describes a universal flood and the building of a boat designed to survive it. What was the relationship of these ancient tales to the story related in the Book of Genesis? Was the Genesis narrative based on these stories? Did these stories represent a distorted version of the facts, which were faithfully and accurately preserved in the Genesis narrative alone? We begin to deal with these questions by describing in outline some of these ancient Near Eastern stories.

In the Sumerian King List (which some date from about 2000 BC) we find a list of kings who ruled the various Mesopotamian cities, such as Eridu and Shuruppak. In it we find a reference to a flood: "These are five cities, eight kings ruled them for 241,000 years. Then the flood swept over the earth." This Sumerian literature also presents us with Ziusudra, an ancient ruler of the city of Shuruppak. In this story the gods decide to flood the world to destroy mankind. The god Enki warns Zuisudra to build a large boat. He complies and builds the boat. A storm brings rain for seven days. After the flood, Zuisudra is taken to dwell in Dilmun, at the place of the rising of the sun.

In the Akkadian epic of *Atrahasis,* the gods determine to destroy the human race. They try to reduce the noisy population by sending plague, famine, and drought; when all this fails, they try to destroy it by sending a flood. The ruler of Shuruppak is warned of the coming flood and told to build a boat to survive it. He does so, bringing his goods onto the boat, as well as animals. At the end of the *Atrahasis* story, the gods decide to keep the human population down by a combination of sterility, miscarriage, and demons who snatch the babies from their mothers' laps.

In the Old Babylonian *Epic of Gilgamesh*, we find yet another story of the flood. The gods have become weary of men, for their noise was overwhelming, keeping them from sleep, so they resolve to destroy the earth by sending a flood to keep the noise down. A certain Utnapishtim, the man of Shuruppak, is warned by his god that a flood is coming upon the world. He builds a boat in seven days and into it brings his family, his silver and gold, and craftsmen. The ship is larger than the ark in the Genesis narrative, being a cube of 120 cubits and containing seven decks. At the end of the flood, Utnapishtim sends out from the boat a dove, then a swallow, then a raven. When eventually he comes safely to land, he offers a sacrifice to the gods. At the end, Utnapishtim and his wife are taken to reside far away at the mouth of the rivers, being given eternal life like the gods.

The overlapping details between these stories (especially the *Epic of Gilgamesh*) and the Genesis narrative are too similar to be entirely coincidental. Could it be that these other stories are cultural echoes of an historical flood? What is the historicity undergirding this consistent Near Eastern tradition? Was there a universal flood to which these varied tales bear witness? We begin by thinking about what a universal flood covering the entire globe to a height above its mountaintops would have meant.

Scientifically, such a flood would have been impossible. It has been estimated[18] that to cover Mount Ararat (whose peak stands at about 17,000 feet) the sea would have had to rise approximately 17,000 feet all over the globe, requiring an extra 630 million cubic

---

18 The figures and reflections presented throughout this section are from Walton, John H., NIV Application Commentary, *Genesis* (Grand Rapids, MI: Zondervan, 2001), pp. 322f.

miles of water. That is, the sea would have had to triple its volume in only 150 days. Then, all this extra water would have had to recede back to its original level, all in a very short period of time. Where could this water have come from? Where did it go? The rain clouds cannot hold a tenth of one percent of the water necessary to cover the globe as described in our narrative.

It is because of this that some posit not a universal flood covering the globe, but a regional flood that covered a large area in Mesopotamia. These interpreters harmonize such a flood with the biblical text by asserting that in Noah's day all the population of the world was still confined to Mesopotamia—as presumably were all the world's birds and animals. Certainly this would explain the comparative absence of any traditions of a universal flood in such places as Africa,[19] but certain other logistical difficulties still remain. If seven pairs of every clean animal and bird were brought aboard the ark, this would amount to about 42,000 creatures. One wonders how such a staggering collection would fit and survive in a small space for about a year (the duration of their stay according to the biblical record; see Gen. 7:11; 8:13–14). How would eight people care for them? Clean them? Feed them? Presumably they were not all hibernating, for Noah was instructed to bring along their food (Gen. 6:21). What did the carnivores such as the lions eat? Where did enough fresh water come from to care for them throughout the year?

The problems previously mentioned regarding a universal deluge obtain here too, for if Mount Ararat were covered with water in a mere 150 days and the waters receded soon after, we still may ask where such a volume of water came from and where it went.[20] Even the harmless dove presents us with a problem, for if it was sent from

---

19   Ibid.
20   Difficulties remain even if we posit the ark not settling on the heights of the Ararat range but somewhere in the smaller foothills.

the ark atop Mount Ararat, that meant it would have had to fly down to the lowlands and back from a height of 17,000 feet. Doves are not physically built for mountainous heights.

For all these reasons, we may want to revisit how we read this sacred text. I suggest that we read it as we read the preceding chapters—namely as ancient Near Eastern literature. Certainly these texts in the Book of Genesis are Holy Scripture, produced by the inspiration of God. But, like the rest of Scripture, they should be interpreted according to their literary genre. That means reading them as they would have originally been read by those who first received them.

Stories of an ancient flood were common throughout the ancient Near East. The *Epic of Gilgamesh*, for example, is primarily a series of hero legends. The information it gives about Gilgamesh cannot be considered historically reliable (though scholars have established that there was indeed an historical Gilgamesh who reigned in Uruk during the first half of the third millennium).[21] The point of the story was not the history, but the heroism. It is the same with this narrative. It contains a theme common in its day, telling the story of the ancient flood that swept over the world. But like the *Epic of Gilgamesh*, the focus of our story is not on history, but on heroism—or rather on power, judgment, and redemption, for the story's main protagonist is not Noah, but God. In its inspired retelling of a cultural commonplace, the sacred author incorporates the story into his epic narrative of God's creation and makes certain changes as he does so. It is these changes and these emphases that constitute the main point of the story.

For example, in the pagan versions of the flood story, the gods sent the flood to obliterate mankind because they had become too

---

21 *The Epic of Gilgamesh: An English Version with an Introduction* by N.K. Sandars (Baltimore: Penguin Books, 1962), p. 20.

populous and thus too noisy, and the gods could not sleep properly. In contrast to such all-too-human deities, who are motivated solely by considerations of their own comfort, Yahweh is transcendent. Human noise does not disturb Him. Rather His concern is with human sin and the injustice and suffering His creations are inflicting upon themselves. His concern is ethical, not self-regarding. The Flood is sent as a judgment upon sin.

That explains another divergence from the pagan versions of the flood story: the person who escaped the judgment did so because of his righteousness. Noah's survival was not the result of accident or divine favoritism but of his blamelessness in his generation (Gen. 6:9). This reveals something fundamental about all the stories of Genesis when compared to the stories of the pagan societies around them—that the God of the Hebrews demanded not simply sacrifices, but righteousness, mercy, and justice from those who worshipped Him. In changing the detail of why the Flood came upon the world and why one man escaped it, the author of the story ethicizes religion. Religion concerns not simply sacrifice, as if the gods needed care and feeding, but righteousness of life. The Noah story is part of the scriptural revolution in how Man should regard God.

Another divergence of the scriptural version from the pagan ones concerns the reaction of God to the Flood. In the *Epic of Gilgamesh*, for example, we read that "even the gods were terrified at the flood; they fled to the highest heaven . . . they crouched against the walls cowering like curs. . . . The great gods of heaven and of hell wept, they covered their mouths."[22] The contrast in the story of Noah is stark, for God reigns sovereignly over the Flood even as He did over the original chaos. Yahweh never cowers.

We see another contrast between our sacred narrative and those of the pagans in the behavior of the gods after the flood has subsided

---

22 *Epic of Gilgamesh*, op. cit., pp. 110–111.

THE RETURN OF CHAOS

and the occupant of the boat has emerged and offered sacrifice. No sacrifices of course had been offered during the week of the deluge, and the gods were hungry after their week of fasting. Thus after the sacrifice was offered, "when the gods smelled the sweet savor, they gathered like flies over the sacrifice."[23] Compare this to Yahweh's serene reaction: "When Yahweh smelled the restful smell, Yahweh said in his heart, 'I will never again humble the ground because of man'" (Gen. 8:21). The gods of the nations were needy and required food from man; Yahweh needs nothing, and Himself provides man with all that he needs. This tiny diverging detail also witnesses to the revolution that was the religion of Israel.

Finally, from the *Atrahasis* story: After the flood, the gods decided to deal with subsequent human overpopulation by sending sterility and miscarriage to keep down the population—which was sensible, the gods doubtless thought, since they judged overpopulation to be the main problem. In contrast, after the Flood in the Noah story, Yahweh actually commands mankind to multiply and to be fruitful. In the pagan versions, the problem was overpopulation and the solution, sterility and miscarriage. In our version, the problem is sin, and the solution, God's patience and mercy—and (placing the Noah story within the larger context of the entirety of the Scriptures) the creation of a chosen people and a Church. How would God ultimately solve the problem of sin? Through Jesus Christ, whose coming was the ultimate goal of the calling of Abraham and the creation of God's people Israel.

Is there then no historicity to this story? The story's value and place in the Scriptures do not depend upon its historicity, but we can nonetheless offer an opinion. I suggest that there was indeed a large-scale catastrophic flood in the ancient Near East, which

---

23 Ibid, p. 111.

functioned as the cultural catalyst for all these stories.[24] How the stories took shape depended upon the various cultures and values and religions in which they were found. Our story took shape in order to express the divine values God was revealing to Israel. We may sit lightly upon the details of the tale (details such as the duration of the Flood, the mountaintops being covered, the number of animals gathered, and the extent of the destruction). Receiving the story as Scripture brings with it the obligation to view it not as historically reliable in its details, but only as morally binding in its theology.

A final note may be added about the New Testament appropriation of the Noah story. The writers of the first century had no reason to inquire about issues of historicity, and so they simply assumed the accuracy of the story. But the use these writers made of the story was independent of the story's historicity. Christ used it as a literary comparison for the suddenness of His Second Coming, saying that as the people in the Noah story were unprepared for judgment, so will the world be unprepared when He comes again (Matt. 24:37f). St. Peter found in the story a type and foreshadowing of Christian baptism, for just as Noah came through the water and left behind the old world of sin to enter a new world washed clean, so the Christian emerges from the baptismal waters, leaving behind the old life of sin to enter the new world of the Kingdom of God (1 Pet. 3:20–21). None of the truths the New Testament offers rely on the historical accuracy of Noah's epic tale.

---

24 Some suggest that Fara, the site of ancient Shuruppak, gives archaeological evidence of a deluge; see Sarna, Nahum M., JPS Torah Commentary, *Genesis* (Philadelphia: JPS Society, 1989), p. 48.

CHAPTER 5

Rebellion and Dispersal

Building the Tower and Spreading over the Earth

Though this section begins with the words **These are the generations of the sons of Noah, Shem, Ham, and Japheth**, giving the impression that what follows will be simply more family history (Heb. *toldoth*), what in fact follows is unparalleled in the literature of the ancient Near East. Chapter ten consists not of history and straightforward genealogy so much as a geographical snapshot of the world as seen from the perspective of Israel in the first millennium before Christ.

Some of the names in the genealogy refer to individuals (e.g., Eber and Nimrod), some refer to places and nations (e.g., Cush and Egypt), some refer to cities (e.g., Sidon), and some refer to peoples (e.g., the Jebusites and Girgashites). When one couples this with the observation that the list contains seventy names, one may safely conclude that the author here offers more than simple genealogy. The number seventy symbolized totality, and so this list, selective as it is, symbolized all the nations of the world known to Israel at that time.

Further, by declaring in Genesis 46:27 and Exodus 1:5 that when Israel entered Egypt they numbered seventy persons, the text prepares us to see Israel as a microcosm of the world. That is, the world's fate depended on Israel, because the Creator of the world was Israel's God, and He had chosen Israel to be His instrument of revelation and redemption. We Christians know the further detail that Israel became the instrument of world redemption through its Messiah, the One through whom all the nations of the world were blessed (Gen. 12:3; Gal. 3:8, 14).

In this snapshot of the world, the author traces all the nations of the world back to the sons of Noah, thereby declaring all men to be brothers and fellow members of the human family—a revolutionary concept in those days, when each nation considered foreign nations to be barbarians unequal to themselves. The author also declares that all the nations of the world are beholden to Israel's God, the One who saved Noah and his sons from the Flood, allowing these nations to come into being in the first place. Theology—indeed, polemical theology—here dresses itself in the garments of genealogy.

This may provide a clue regarding the chronology of the narrative and why the author provides us with a list of the dispersed nations of the earth before narrating the story of how the nations came to be dispersed in the first place (the story of the tower of Babel). The Babel story in the next chapter relates how mankind came to be dispersed over the far corners of the earth as part of God's judgment. A more strictly chronological approach would have narrated that story first and then listed the various nations and the places to which they were dispersed. But such an approach would have put primary stress on the fact of their dispersal, while the narrator desired to place the primary stress on their underlying unity. This could only be done by connecting them closely to the **sons** of Shem, Ham, and Japheth who **were born to them after the flood**. Following a stricter chronology and inserting the story of the tower of Babel between the birth of Noah's descendants and the list of where they were eventually to be found would have weakened this crucial connection. For the author, chronology must serve theology.

10 These are the generations of the sons of Noah, Shem, Ham, and Japheth. Sons were born to them after the flood.

[2] The sons of Japheth: Gomer, Magog, Madai, Javan, Tubal, Meshech, and Tiras. [3] The sons of Gomer: Ashkenaz, Riphath, and Togarmah. [4] The sons of Javan: Elishah, Tarshish, Kittim, and Rodanim. [5] From these the coastland nations spread in their lands, each with his own language, by their clans, in their nations.

[6] The sons of Ham: Cush, Egypt, Put, and Canaan. [7] The sons of Cush: Seba, Havilah, Sabtah, Raamah, and Sabteca. The sons of Raamah: Sheba and Dedan. [8] Cush fathered Nimrod; he was the first on earth to be a warrior. [9] He was a mighty hunter before Yahweh. Therefore it is said, "Like Nimrod a mighty hunter before Yahweh." [10] The beginning of his kingdom was Babel, Erech, Akkad, all of them[25] in the land of Shinar. [11] From that land he went into Assyria and built Nineveh, the open places of the city, Calah, and [12] Resen between Nineveh and Calah; that is the great city. [13] Egypt fathered Ludim, Anamim, Lehabim, Naphtuhim, [14] Pathrusim, Casluhim (from whom the Philistines came), and Caphtorim.

[15] Canaan fathered Sidon his firstborn and Heth, [16] and the Jebusites, the Amorites, the Girgashites, [17] the Hivites, the Arkites, the Sinites, [18] the Arvadites, the Zemarites, and the Hamathites. Afterward the clans of the Canaanites dispersed. [19] And the territory of the Canaanites extended from Sidon in the direction of Gerar as far as Gaza, and in the direction of Sodom, Gomorrah, Admah, and Zeboiim, as far as Lasha. [20] These are the sons of Ham, by their clans, their languages, their lands, and their nations.

[21] To Shem also, the father of all the sons of Eber, brother of the older Japheth, sons were born. [22] The sons of Shem: Elam, Assyria, Arpachshad, Lud, and Aram. [23] The sons of Aram: Uz, Hul, Gether, and Mash. [24] Arpachshad fathered Shelah; and Shelah fathered

---

25   Reading *Calneh* as a phrase, not another city.

Eber. ²⁵ To Eber were born two sons: the name of the one was Peleg, for in his days the earth was divided, and his brother's name was Joktan. ²⁶ Joktan fathered Almodad, Sheleph, Hazarmaveth, Jerah, ²⁷ Hadoram, Uzal, Diklah, ²⁸ Obal, Abimael, Sheba, ²⁹ Ophir, Havilah, and Jobab; all these were the sons of Joktan. ³⁰ The dwelling in which they lived extended from Mesha in the direction of Sephar to the hill country of the east. ³¹ These are the sons of Shem, by their clans, their languages, their lands, and their nations.

³² These are the clans of the sons of Noah, according to their generations, in their nations, and from these the nations spread out on the earth after the flood.

The sons of Noah are enumerated as usual as **Shem, Ham, and Japheth**, but the author reverses this order when listing their descendants, listing first the **sons of Japheth**, then **the sons of Ham**, and finally **the sons of Shem**. This was deliberate, for it put Shem in the final position as the culmination and crown of God's purpose for the nations. It was from Shem's line that Israel would come.

The author listed as **the sons of Japheth** seven sons (another symbolic number, denoting totality). **Gomer** corresponds to the Cimmerians near the Black Sea in what was later Cappadocia. **Magog** may well represent a people in Anatolia. The **Madai** were the Medes, who may have arrived in what is now Iran by 1000 BC. **Javan** represented Ionian Greece. **Tubal** and **Meshech** have been located in Anatolia. Less certainty attaches to **Tiras**, which may represent one of the sea peoples who attacked Egypt in the thirteenth century.

The author then focuses on the line of **Gomer**, listing the groups tracing themselves back to him as **Ashkenaz** (i.e., the Ashkuza, the Scythians), **Riphath** (possibly the Paphlagonians who lived near Bithynia), and **Togarmah** (which may represent Tegarama, a city between Assyria and Kanish).

Next the author listed the line of **Javan**, enumerated as **Elishah**, **Tarshish**, **Kittim**, and **Rodanim**. **Elishah** and **Kittim** are thought to be on the island of Cyprus. **Tarshish** may be far away west of Gibraltar or (more likely) someplace closer, such as Carthage in Phoenicia. The reading **Rodanim** is to be preferred to "Dodanim"; the former is the reading of the Septuagint. It denoted the inhabitants of Rhodes. The final referent **these** in verse 5 seems to denote all the sons of Japheth, rather than just the sons of Javan. If this is so, the author thought of Japhath as **the coastland nations**—those living in the coastlines and faraway places. The term "coastlands" in the Scriptures always has connotations of distance (see for example Is. 41:5, where "the coastlands" parallels "the ends of the earth").

The next major grouping was that of the **sons of Ham**, four in number: **Cush**, **Egypt**, **Put**, and **Canaan**. **Cush** is commonly considered to be south of Egypt, around Ethiopia (which is how the Septuagint usually translates the term), though some suggest a location in Midian. Others suggest a connection with the Cassites. If **Put** is considered to be a Libyan tribe west of **Egypt**,[26] then a location for Cush south of Egypt may seem more likely. **Canaan** obviously refers to our present Holy Land, which had close connections with Egypt as one of its provinces. This might explain why the author lists the Canaanites as Hamite rather than (as one might expect) Semitic sons of Shem—the connection is one of geopolitics, not race.

The author then lists the lines of the sons of Ham (all except Put, for whom no further line is given). First come the **sons of Cush,** listed as **Seba**, **Havilah**, **Sabtah**, **Raamah**, and **Sabteca**, most of which may be located in Arabia. The author then follows one of these, **Raamah**, listing **Sheba** and **Dedan,** both of which were in Arabia, as branching off from this line.

---

26 The Hebrew term for Egypt is *Mizraim*, a dual noun denoting both Upper and Lower Egypt.

The author next considers **Nimrod, fathered** by **Cush**. Nimrod is evidently of some importance to the narrative, for the author spends much time on him and his career. He was the first on earth to be **a warrior** (Heb. *gibbor*)—that is, a person of immense political power. Nimrod was further described as providing the popular paradigm of being **a mighty hunter**, and his career began in **Babel** (Babylon), **Erech** (Uruk in Sumer), and **Akkad** (Agade, the capital city of Sargon), all of them **in the land of Shinar**, or Sumer. From there **Nimrod went into Assyria and built Nineveh**, with **the open places of the city,**[27] as well as the neighboring cities of **Calah** and **Resen**.

Scholars can find no consensus for an historical identification of Nimrod. One suggestion identifies him with the Assyrian king Tukulti-Ninurta I, who reigned from about 1246 BC and was the first Assyrian king to reign over both Assyria and Babylon. Another suggests the historical Gilgamesh as the biblical Nimrod. Yet another suggests Hammurabi. (These identifications assume that the term "Cush" here refers to the Cassites, not to a kingdom south of Egypt.)

Nimrod certainly seems to have been identified with the area of Assyria (compare Micah 5:6, which describes Assyria as "the land of Nimrod"). Perhaps it is best to regard Nimrod as a composite character, representing the father of all proud tyrants and pagan superpowers in the Middle East.

Returning to the list of the sons of Ham, the author focuses on Egypt, listing his sons as the peoples of the **Ludim**, the **Anamim**, the **Lehabim**, the **Naphtuhim**, the **Pathrusim**, the **Casluhim**, and the **Caphtorim**—seven in all, again probably symbolic of totality. The locations of these peoples is not certain. The **Ludim** may be the Lydians in Asia Minor; the **Lehabim** were probably the Libyans;

---

27 Reading *Rehoboth-Ir* (lit., "open spaces") as description, not as the name of another city.

the **Pathrusim** were those from Pathros, in southern Egypt. The **Casluhim** may have been in northern Egypt. The **Caphtorim** were the Cretans or those from an island nearby. It seems as if **the Philistines** originally came to Egypt from Crete.

Finally in the list of Ham's sons, our author lists the children of **Canaan**. These are listed as **Sidon** (the famous Phoenician city) and **Heth**, the founder of the Hittites, who flourished in Asia Minor. The author then lists many of the groups Israel had to displace when they conquered the Promised Land: the **Jebusites**, the **Amorites**, the **Girgashites**, and the **Hivites** (compare Joshua 9:7; 24:11). The **Arvadites** were from Arvad, a Phoenician city; the **Hamathites** were from Hamath, north of Damascus on the Orontes River. These tribes are portrayed as spreading down from the north as far south as **Gaza** and toward **Sodom** and **Gomorrah** near the Dead Sea as far as **Lasha** (possibly Callirhoe, east of the Dead Sea).

Finally, the author comes to what for him is the culmination of this table of nations, the sons of Shem. **Shem** is described as **brother of the older Japheth** (i.e. Japheth was the firstborn, not Shem).[28] The examination of the lines of Shem begins with highlighting Shem's connection with **the sons of Eber**, though Eber will come later down the line (Shem fathers **Arpachshad**, who fathers **Shelah**, who fathers **Eber**). Clearly Eber was of some importance, since he was the ancestor of the Hebrews.

The sons of Shem are listed as **Elam** (the country to the east of Israel's world), **Assyria** (the city of Asshur, the old capital of the Assyrian country), **Arpachshad** (possibly modern Kirkuk in Iraq), the city of **Uz** in northwestern Mesopotamia, **Lud**, and **Aram**. This last may refer to a settlement east of Assyria. Going down the

---

28   This follows the reading of the Septuagint. It is grammatically possible to read this as "Shem, the older brother of Japheth," making Shem the firstborn. See comment on Gen. 11:10.

lines of the generations, the author mentions that **Archpachshad** fathered **Shelah,** who fathered **Eber,** who fathered both **Peleg** and **Joktan.**

In an historical note, the author mentions that **Peleg** was so named **for in his days the earth was divided** (for *peleg* means "division"). But what division was this? Some suggest it refers to the division and confusion that came as divine judgment for building the tower of Babel (compare Ps. 55:9, which uses the same verb: "divide their tongues"). Others connect the verb with the Akkadian *palgu,* or "canal," and suggest that the reference credits Peleg with the creation of irrigation canals, but if this were so one might have expected the author to speak of the *adamah* or "ground" being divided, not the "earth" (Heb. *eretz*).

Peleg's brother **Joktan** fathered thirteen sons, most of whom can be connected with Arabia and Yemen. They were spread out from **Mesha** (in northern Arabia) to **Sephar.** The meaning of this last word is uncertain; it may indicate a town in the southern Arabian coast.

With this list the author reaches his conclusion and sums it all up by adding **these are the clans of the sons of Noah . . . and from these the nations spread out on the earth after the flood.** By referring once again to Noah and the Flood, the author presents Noah as the new fountainhead of humanity. All the many and varied nations, wherever they may have been throughout the wide earth, owed their existence to Noah's obedience to Yahweh—and ultimately to Yahweh Himself, who saved Noah. If it were not for Noah, none of these nations would have existed; all would have perished in the Flood.

The table of nations contains some puzzles, such as why Canaan was listed not with Shem but with Ham, and why the Elamites, whose language was not Semitic, *would* be listed with Shem. But if geographical and historical puzzles remain, the basic message is clear: The history of Abraham and Israel is placed squarely in the center of the world and of God's purposes for mankind. Israel's destiny was not a tiny sideshow on the fringes of historical significance, despite the nation's small size and lack of worldly power. Israel stood firmly in direct linear succession to what the Creator and Judge of the world was doing in the earth.

11 Now the whole earth had one language and the same words. ² And as they travelled from the east, they found a plain in the land of Shinar and settled there. ³ And they said to one another, "Come, let us make bricks and burn them thoroughly." And they had brick for stone and bitumen for mortar. ⁴ Then they said, "Come, let us build ourselves a city and a tower with its head in the heavens, and let us make a name for ourselves, lest we be dispersed over the face of the whole earth." ⁵ And Yahweh came down to see the city and the tower, which the sons of man had built. ⁶ And Yahweh said, "Behold, they are one people, and they have all one language, and this is only the beginning of what they will do. And nothing that they propose to do will now be impossible for them. ⁷ Come, let us go down and there confuse their language, so that they may not understand one another's speech." ⁸ So Yahweh dispersed them from there over the face of all the earth, and they left off building the city. ⁹ Therefore its name was called Babel, because there Yahweh confused the language of all the earth. And from there Yahweh dispersed them over the face of all the earth.

Just as the narrator connected the multiplication of the human race (in the genealogy in chapter five) with an increase of sin (in the stories of Cain and the Flood in chapters four and six), so he does the same thing here. The narrator connects the story of mankind's multiplication (in the table of nations in chapter ten) with the story of mankind's sinful rebellion (in the story of the tower in chapter eleven). The message is all too clear: Mankind continued to multiply and grow strong and become ever more technologically glorious in its arts and power, but at the same time mankind continued to rebel against God. The human race had become strong, but its strength turned its heart to pride. The story of human history was thus the story of a prodigal son wandering from home, the tale of a race going badly astray. God was in His heaven, but all was not right with the world.

This new tale of rebellion begins with the observation that **the whole earth had one language and the same words**. The author, beginning with a good God creating a good world and placing man in Paradise, has as his destination the world in which we now live, the world of Abraham. The narrative journey has sketched the spreading of the human race throughout the world, and it must now explain how that one race, though proceeding from a single family, came to exhibit such diversity of language, custom, and geography as we now find. The story was not simply an etiological tale, explaining how the various languages came to exist. It was about how the warring world that we experience every day came to exist. The story of the tower of Babel represents the final narrative step in the long, depressing journey from the garden to the world of conflict, idolatry, and power we know so well.

The phenomenon and cause of the diversity of languages seems not to have occupied the ancient myth-makers very much, and there are few literary parallels to our story from that time. We do find one mythical tale reporting that the world once shared the same language, the Sumerian story *Enmerkar and the Lord of Aratta*. In part the poem reads, "Once there was no snake, there was no scorpion . . . there was no fear, no terror; Man had no rival. . . . The whole universe, the people in unison spoke to Enlil in one tongue.

. . . Enki . . . the leader of the gods . . . changed the speech in their mouths and brought contention into it, into the speech of man that until then had been one."[29] In this tale, speech was changed through the rivalry of the gods Enlil and Enki.

Once again the Genesis story takes a different approach. Just as the Flood was caused by the sin of mankind and not by the gods' distress at not being able to sleep for all the noise, so the social confusion caused by diversity of language resulted from human sin, not from divine quarrelling. We created the mess down here; we are the cause of our own misery.

In our story, the people traveled from the east, found a plain in the land of Shinar, and settled there. The geographical detail that the people came **from the east** may represent more than the narrative necessity of bringing them from the mountains of Ararat to Babylon (which would have involved mostly a southward movement). The east in our narrative also represents the far distance—Eden was in the east, and Cain went wandering in the east (Gen. 2:8; 4:16). The reference to men coming from the east may be intended by the author as an image of mankind coming near to his readers' present historical situation from a place now foreign to their experience. The ancient ones left the faraway land of legend to enter the historical world we know. The place they settled was **Shinar**, also called Sumer and Babylonia. In our narrative it is synonymous with idolatry and power. Shinar was the land of Nimrod, the mighty hunter who built Nineveh.

Settling there, they said to one another, **"Come, let us make bricks and burn them thoroughly."** Israel lived in Palestine, a place where stone for building was plentiful. It was otherwise on

---

29 Quoted in Wenham, Gordon J., Word Biblical Commentary, *Genesis 1–15* (Waco, TX: Word Books, 1987), p. 358.

the Mesopotamian plain. There was no stone for building close at hand, and so kiln-fired brickmaking would be required to build a city with a tower, as the author explains to his Israelite audience.

The brickmaking was but part of a larger, more ambitious project: **"Come, let us build ourselves a city and a tower with its head in the heavens."** The double repetition of **"Come, let us"** reinforces the people's determination to **make a name** for themselves. If they were **dispersed over the face of the whole earth,** no one would enjoy individual fame. But by banding together in such a city with such a tower, they would ensure immortal fame for themselves.

Their offense was not in resisting dispersal, for God's command to fill the earth (Gen. 9:1) did not entail the obligation to immediately scatter into different directions. That scattering would come soon enough, as the people multiplied and needed more space. The offense was in seeking to make a name for themselves—that is, finding earthly glory and founding a civilization apart from God. The first man and woman had thought to become gods and seize their own moral autonomy, and they were punished by banishment from their place. The same offense was now being repeated on a large scale, and one could justly expect the same punishment.

The cultural background for the tower was of course the ziggurat. Ziggurats were built as manmade mountains on the flat Mesopotamian plain as homes for the gods. The ziggurat was dedicated to a god and had a ramp or stairway outside it leading up to a little room at the top, furnished with a bed and table, which functioned as a home for the deity to whom it was dedicated. The god was invited and expected to dwell there and from this place bless the people. These were impressive structures. One famous ziggurat in Babylon rose three hundred feet above the ground. The description of the tower of our story as having **its head in the heavens** echoes common descriptions of ziggurats. It did not mean of course that the building literally went up to God's heavenly dwelling, but rather that it functioned as the meeting place between heaven and earth.

Though the ziggurat stood in the background of our story, it would be pressing the cultural background too much to import all the meaning and function of a ziggurat into our narrative. The tower here functions simply as a sign of man's pride, his hubris, his desire for an enduring name. The **tower** was paired with the **city** as the twin expression of man's rebellious desire to build a civilization for his own glory.

It is true, of course, that ziggurats were built precisely to honor and glorify the pagan gods, not as a monument to the glory of man. But our author was not writing history but polemical theology. Those pagan gods for whom the ziggurats were built never put in an appearance in our narrative. In the mythological telling of the story of the city and the tower, our author focuses solely on mankind's rebellion against Yahweh, the only God whom mankind had thus far known. Certainly the building of the ziggurat/tower and the city to surround it would redound to the glory of the builders, and it is this glory that is the focus of our narrative.

Man's pride received an immediate divine response. There is some subtle satire in that response. Man had thought to build a tower so tall that **its head** would be **in the heavens**, but Yahweh is so high above man and his puny plans that He has to come **down** from heaven to even **see the city and the tower**. When He saw what mankind had done, He reached a conclusion (signaled by a dramatic **behold**): this project was **only the beginning for them, and nothing that they propose to do will now be impossible for them**. Being **one people** with **one language** meant untold possibilities for them.

The problem was that they were misusing their unity. The unity that was meant to be used for mutual care and kindness and the common worship of Yahweh was now being used to create civilization without reference to Him. They had used their unity to cross a boundary and arrogate to themselves the power to decide their own destiny. In their sinful pride, they could not be trusted to build wisely. Separated from the divine wisdom, their accomplishments and technology could only lead to self-harm and death. Human history seethes with examples proving that men cannot be trusted with power. Even in our divided state, the civilizations we have built have been built over the bones of the slaughtered innocents.

It was ultimately for our own good, therefore, that **Yahweh said to His divine council, "Come, let us go down and there confuse their language."** The double repetition of man saying "Come, let us" finds a single answer from Yahweh, who also says "Come, let us." At a stroke He **confuses their language** so that they cannot **understand one another's speech.** He then **dispersed them from there over all the face of the earth**, so that the very fate man had dreaded and tried to avoid at length came upon them. Thus divided and scattered, **they left off building the city**. It would remain half built, a monument to the folly of prideful disobedience.

The story contains some wordplays in the original Hebrew. In Hebrew the human resolve "let us make" [bricks] in verse 3 is *nil-benah*; the divine answer "let us confuse" in verse 7 is *nabelah*. The confusion sent by God thus undoes the human resolve to build. Another wordplay involves the word for Babel. In its original context, the name for Babylon meant "gate of god," later reflected in the Babylonian name *bab-ili*. The author here heaps scorn on such a pretended divine gate, saying that men now call the place **Babel**, from the Hebrew word *balal*, "to confuse," **because there** at Babel **Yahweh confused the language of all the earth**. There is no actual etymological connection between the two, of course. But the author is not teaching language; he is deriding paganism and exalting Yahweh. For an Israelite, Babel and Babylon could only indicate confusion.

What does this story mean for us today? The author does not offer it as history or as an accurate explanation of why there are so many languages on the earth, and accepting this story as Holy Scripture does not require that we accept it as such. If historians of language offer evidence that there was never a single human language, we are free to listen to them. This story represents the last leg of our journey before coming into the real world of history, when Abraham would leave his country at the command of God. Like the stories that preceded this one, on the plain of Shinar we still live in a land of legend, of historicized myth and mythological history, a place where truths are too big to fit under our modern microscopes. But what is the truth this story offers us?

This story tells us that unity alone is not enough and that it is not a good in itself. Unity that is not rooted in humility before God always ends badly sooner or later. That is why God in His mercy shattered this dark and dangerous unity, dividing mankind into separate nations by dividing their tongues. Mankind's first step down the road of moral autonomy was the founding of a city and the building of a tower. Unless the way down that road were blocked, mankind would continue along it, using its united technology and wisdom to inflict horrendous wounds on the helpless of the earth. This international unity will eventually find expression in the world as it unites around the Antichrist. In that day, the year will always be 1984.

This story therefore warns us that the monuments we build apart from God will not lead to joy. When our first parents disobeyed God, they did not achieve the joy they were implicitly promised, and in the same way technological knowledge apart from humility will never lead to joy. Achieving mastery over the atom did not bring unmixed blessing but formed clouds of death over our heads. The presumption and hubris of these first tower builders continues to dwell in human hearts. We have yet to learn that simply because we *can* do something does not mean that we *may* or *should* do it, and the evidence of our blindness and folly surrounds us on every side.

[10] These are the generations of Shem. When Shem was 100 years old, he fathered Arpachshad two years after the flood. [11] And Shem lived after he fathered Arpachshad 500 years and had other sons and daughters.

[12] When Arpachshad had lived 35 years, he fathered Shelah. [13] And Arpachshad lived after he fathered Shelah 403 years and had other sons and daughters.

[14] When Shelah had lived 30 years, he fathered Eber. [15] And Shelah lived after he fathered Eber 403 years and had other sons and daughters.

[16] When Eber had lived 34 years, he fathered Peleg. [17] And Eber lived after he fathered Peleg 430 years and had other sons and daughters.

[18] When Peleg had lived 30 years, he fathered Reu. [19] And Peleg lived after he fathered Reu 209 years and had other sons and daughters.

[20] When Reu had lived 32 years, he fathered Serug. [21] And Reu lived after he fathered Serug 207 years and had other sons and daughters.

[22] When Serug had lived 30 years, he fathered Nahor. [23] And Serug lived after he fathered Nahor 200 years and had other sons and daughters.

[24] When Nahor had lived 29 years, he fathered Terah. [25] And Nahor lived after he fathered Terah 119 years and had other sons and daughters.

²⁶ When Terah had lived 70 years, he fathered Abram, Nahor, and Haran.

With the enumeration of **the generations of Shem**, the narrator finally closes the colorful book of mythology and steps firmly into the realm of history. This progression to the historically accurate world can be gauged even from the numbers used in this final genealogy, for the numbers are still hyperbolic and inflated, but not as much as before (indeed, the ages listed for when their first sons were born may not be inflated at all).

The ancients believed the first men lived fantastically long lives, and so our narrator drew his genealogical picture of them accordingly. But the ancestors of Abraham were not the first men, and so the ages are considerably lower than in the genealogy of chapter five. The ancient Seth lived a total of 912 years (Gen. 5:8), whereas **Shem** died at the age of 600. And after the postdiluvian Shem, the figures drop even more dramatically: **Archpachshad fathered Shelah** at the age of **35 years** (compare **Shem's** first child when he was **100 years old**), dying at the age of 438. Continuing the drop in lifespan, we read that **Serug** was **30 years old** when he **fathered Nahor**, and Serug died at the age of 230. The drop in numbers tells us that we are hurtling toward history. It seems as if our author has taken the reliable genealogy of Abram and inserted into the previous semi-historical narrative he has been relating, adding another five generations (Reu, Serug, Nahor, Terah, and Abram) to the previous five generations (Shem, Arpachshad, Shelah, Eber, and Peleg).

The positions of the persons in this list is not accidental or insignificant. Just as Noah came tenth on the list of generations from Adam (Gen. 5:28), so Abram comes tenth on the list from Shem. The mathematical message would be clear to the ancient audience: just as Noah had a special, defining, and saving role in the world that emerged from Adam, so Abram would have a similar role in the world that emerged from Shem after the Flood.

The text contains a few puzzles. As with the numbers of the ages for the genealogy in chapter five, the numbers of this list also vary between the Hebrew Masoretic text, the Samaritan Pentateuch, and the Greek Septuagint. Most scholars follow the Hebrew Masoretic as more likely to be reliable. Also, the Septuagint text inserts the name Cainan after that of Archpachshad, so that Archpachshad directly begot not Shelah but Cainan; it was Cainan who begot Shelah. (St. Luke, who used the Septuagint, followed this reading in his genealogy for Jesus in Luke 3:23f.) The addition is probably not original, for the numbers given for Cainan at the birth of his first son and at his death are identical to those of Shelah that follow him, and it looks as if a redactor simply borrowed the numbers from Shelah for his additional Cainan. Also, the addition of Cainan to the list destroys the parallelism of ten generations from Adam to Noah and from post-Flood Shem to Abram. For these reasons, the Hebrew list is preferred.

Another puzzle revolves around Shem's age at the birth of Arpachshad. In Genesis 5:32 we read that when Noah was 500 years old, he became the father of Shem, Ham, and Japheth. Obviously, all three sons couldn't have been born in the same year (unless they were triplets, which would surely have been remarked upon)—so which one was born when Noah was 500 years old? Given the priority of Shem in most of the lists (e.g., 6:10, which reads, "Noah had three sons, Shem, Ham, and Japheth"), many suppose Shem to be the eldest, the one born during Noah's five-hundredth year. Some find confirmation of this in Genesis 10:21, if the reading is adopted making Shem the older brother of Japheth. By Noah's six-hundredth year, the year of the Flood (Gen. 7:11), the eldest, Shem, would have been 100 years old.

But if that is true, then how are we to understand Genesis 11:10, which states that **Shem fathered Arpachshad** when he **was 100 years old,** *two years after the flood?* For if Shem was born in Noah's five-hundredth year, then Shem was 100 years old when the Flood came and 102 years old two years after the Flood. The puzzle is solved if we make *Japheth* the eldest son, born when Noah was 500 years old (consistent with the Septuagint reading of Gen. 10:21), with Shem born two years after Japheth. That would indeed make Shem 98 when the Flood came and 102 two years after the Flood, as the text here states. (It is the birth order, and not the precise numbers, that is of concern here.)

These brief **generations** or family histories come to an end with the notation that **Terah fathered Abram, Nahor, and Haran.** The purpose of recounting the long epic stretching from the creation of the world to a migration from Ur has been fulfilled, though it had to utilize myth, symbol, and legend to accomplish such a lofty goal. When the author has recourse to "the generations of Terah" (Gen. 11:27f) to tell the story of Abraham, he can safely lay aside the tools of mythology. Terah with his family strides out of Ur onto the world stage, carrying a destiny they could little imagine.

CONCLUSION

Remembering Who We Are

We LIVE IN A TIME of spiritual amnesia, subject to forces in our culture that cause us to forget who we actually are and what it means to live as an authentic human person. If the fourth century was the time when God called the Church to defend its apostolic Christology, the twenty-first century is the time when the Church is being called to defend its apostolic anthropology. In the fourth century, heretics offered a distorted view of who Jesus of Nazareth was. We now face forces that promote a distorted view of human nature itself. We have forgotten what authentic human nature looks like. We have forgotten who we are.

This is not the first time God's people have struggled to overcome a false view of their true nature and calling. In the time of the prophet Isaiah, God's people also had forgotten who they were. They believed they belonged to the Baals and to the multitude of false gods on whom they imagined their prosperity and security depended. They forgot that they belonged to Yahweh, the God who made a covenant with the patriarchs, brought them out of Egypt, gave them His Law, and settled them in Canaan.

Isaiah therefore said to them, "Look to the rock from which you were hewn, and to the quarry from which you were dug. Look to Abraham your father and to Sarah who bore you" (Is. 51:1–2). That is, through the prophet, God reminded Israel of their true origins and identity as His covenant people. That prophetic reminder was the divine voice calling them home to safety, sanity, and salvation.

The idolatrous culture around them gave them no help in understanding who they were and how they should live, for it told them that the gods of Canaan were the ones to worship if they wanted to succeed. Israel needed to look away from the lies of the present and learn the lessons from the past. Only in knowing how they all began could they know who they really were and how they should live.

In the same way, our own secular culture today provides no help in understanding who we really are or what kind of behavior flows from authentic human nature and promotes authentic spiritual health. We too need to look to the rock from which we were hewn and the quarry from which we were dug. We need to turn once again to the origin stories of the Book of Genesis to learn the truth about what it means to be an authentic human being. The Genesis narrative teaches us lessons about human nature we cannot learn from the secular society around us. Which lessons? We conclude by mentioning four of them.

1. Human Life Is Sacred

First of all, these origin stories remind us that all human life is sacred. By employing language once reserved for royalty in describing man and woman as being made in God's image, the sacred author elevates the value of every human being. This was revolutionary in the ancient world, where (to borrow the famous description of Thomas Hobbes) life was nasty, brutish, mean, and short. Given this, it is not surprising that human life was cheap.

Despite our modern boasting in the West that we now value human life in a way that sets us apart from previous barbaric ages, it may be doubted whether our "progressive" culture has really progressed much at all. Every year, for example, we slaughter the unborn, disposing of their corpses as if they were so much garbage.

Large portions of the general population in the West are committed to maintaining a woman's access to paid professionals who will murder her unborn child for her as if this were her inalienable right. In my own country of Canada, this supposed right has become so entrenched in our culture and is so jealously guarded and protected that public debate over it is scarcely possible, and two of the three major political parties have enshrined it as part of their platform. And the third party will not allow the topic to arise, recognizing that to speak against state-funded abortion is political suicide.

The Genesis narrative comes to us as a standing protest against such slaughter, for it proclaims that each person comes into the world bearing the royal image of our God and King. Absolutely everyone living bears this image. The unborn baby bears it equally with his older siblings and his parents. The mentally challenged bear it equally with the brilliant; the poor man bears it equally with the rich. The young, dynamic, and socially useful have no advantage here over the old, spent, and apparently useless. The ones suffering the ravages of Alzheimer's disease have the same value before God as the doctors treating them and striving to find their cure. All human life is valuable, regardless of recognized social utility or the lack of it. Simply being human brings with it a hidden and irrevocable dignity.

Feeding the poor, therefore, is not charity but justice, for it discerns within the humblest beggar the shining divine image God has implanted in everyone. This is why sin is so terrible and so heartbreaking. It is foreign to our true natures; it distorts and debases something beautiful. Living a life of righteousness and sanctity does not make anyone heroic; it simply makes us human, for holiness is the state in which human beings were meant to live. The origin stories of Genesis remind us that God made every human being in His image, and therefore all life is precious.

2. All Men Are Brothers

Secondly, the Genesis narrative declares that all men are brothers. This truth, often accepted in theory, quickly becomes submerged as the passions rise, fueled by conflicts based on race, tribe, nationalism, or religion. In America many struggle with issues of racism, and throughout the wider world people label other tribes, nations, and religions as "the enemy" and wage bitter war against them. Cain still slays his brother, and that blood still cries out to God from the ground. Rage and murder define us as a species, and through all human history murder has never ceased. Think about it: someone somewhere in the world is being murdered *right now*. Little wonder that the sacred author chose to begin the tale of life outside Paradise with fratricide; fratricide is what we do.

The origin stories set our feet on a better path. They remind us that, in the later words of St. Paul, "God made from one man every nation of men to live on all the face of the earth" (Acts 17:26), and it matters little whether by "one man" Paul referred to Adam or Noah. The truth remains the same either way—we are all literally brothers, members of the same human family. We are children of one mother, for Adam's wife became the mother of all the living.

This is the truth tucked away in the long genealogies of the early chapters of Genesis. No matter what our religion, tribe, or nation, regardless of whether we can trace our line to Shem, Ham, or Japheth, all people come from one and the same man—that is, we are all of one and the same race. Skin color has nothing to do with it, for the only color that really matters is red—the color all people bleed when they are hurt and dying. By remembering that all men are brothers, we can resist and master sin, which crouches at our door (Gen. 4:7); we can refuse to allow diversity to harden into division. The name of the person standing across from us (possibly on the other side of a military no-man's-land) is Abel. The

Genesis narrative teaches that we do not need to rise up and slay our brother.

3. Women Are Precious

Thirdly, these origin stories also remind us of how precious women are, for in their narrative the *adam* instantly recognized the woman as *ishah*, as his completion, as his own flesh and bone. In this epiphany he knew woman to be a divine gift, given to him from the hand of God Himself, and thus of inestimable worth.

Whatever our culture's rhetoric concerning the advances brought about by feminism, it still has much to learn. Our land is awash in pornography; the use of it is increasing, and children are now exposed to it at ever younger ages. Moreover, its use is rapidly becoming normalized; some now speak of their porn collection in the same way as in previous ages one might have spoken of one's stamp collection.

In this universe, women (and often children) are treated as a commodity; they are not valued as persons but simply as flesh for sale. That is why women in pornographic images and in the sex trade are essentially nameless: the buyer does not care for the person but the body. And after the flesh has been bought and used, the buyer retains no interest in the woman herself. Large segments of our culture connive at this devaluation of women and even seek to legitimize the practice of prostitution as somehow empowering for women. (Sanitizing language is always the first step: prostitutes are now often referred to not as prostitutes, but as "sex trade workers.")

The origin stories contradict this cultural erosion of feminine worth. The body of a woman must be respected because it is the instrument through which God continues to create the world. The first man knew this and called the woman "Life." Recognizing the worth of women and the sanctity of feminine gifts means that pornography is not only sinful; it is essentially sacrilegious as well, for it demeans and denigrates the gifts of God. Women are worthy of veneration and respect simply because they are women, and in saner ages a man would arise and remove his hat in the presence of a woman as he would in the presence of his King.

Internalizing this truth about human nature would alter much in our culture, for then men would not treat women as objects or even rivals. Men would know that each woman is a gift, a sign and promise that God still calls the human race to share in the task of creation. Gallantry then becomes not a quaint and quixotic relic of an earlier age or an anachronistic throwback to the Middle Ages. Gallantry is simply the recognition on the part of the man of woman's true worth as God's gift. A man might arise and remove his hat or hold the door open for a particular woman, but the symbolic gesture is really intended for all womankind and as a thanksgiving to God.

4. Gender Is Binary

Finally, these origin stories also remind us that gender is binary. God Himself made mankind as male and female, and for this reason gender is an irrevocable gift, an abiding constant, and not a choice. In teaching this, the Genesis narrative places us upon a collision course with powerful forces and trends in our society. It now appears that the single and defining issue of our generation is that of gender.

In surveying the past half-century or so, we can trace a certain development, like the progression of dementia. It began with seeing the relationship between man and wife in terms of power rather than love. The mutual delight immortalized in such poetry as The Song of Solomon gave way to a view of the sexes as being at war with each other in a perpetual power struggle. In this power struggle, feminists declared that the headship of the husband was inherently oppressive and that gender roles were an all-too-human invention aimed at subverting the rights and dignity of women. In this reconfiguration there was no place for male headship, or indeed for any headship. Egalitarianism was the watchword, and the equality of men and women rapidly came to mean their interchangeability.

This hidden devaluation of gender came to more virulent expression a generation or so later with the rise of what are now called gay rights. Homosexual practice was declared to be as morally legitimate as heterosexuality, and being a homosexual man or a lesbian was deemed not sinful but natural. Open and public declaration of homosexual orientation was applauded and encouraged and was even endowed with the wonderful halo of heroic victimhood. Gender (that is, physical anatomy) now no longer prescribed one's role and choice of sexual partner; men could legitimately have sex with other men and women with women.

Within a few years, society would witness a further stage in the progressive erosion of the traditional understanding of gender, for now an individual could legitimately have sex with both men and women. Previously, homosexual men declared that it was natural for them to be attracted to men but not to women. Now a man can be attracted to and have sex with either gender according to whim.

The present moment witnesses a further development in the ongoing progression, for now some advance the notion that gender itself has no inherent validity. Gender is not a given or a gift but a personal choice. We now are allowed to choose our gender irrespective of our anatomy. This confusion, once regarded by health professionals as a mental pathology, is now labeled as "transgender" and lauded as heroic. Again one witnesses the sanitizing of language: such a confused person now bears the label "gender creative."

Inevitably, the dubious halo of victimhood crowns those who

declare themselves to be "trans," and the struggle to obtain legitimacy for the abolition of gender is portrayed as the noble struggle of the oppressed to obtain their proper rights. The progression away from the timeless and universal norms of gender and marriage has been consistent and seems to have reached its conclusion. If gender itself is simply a subjective choice, there is nothing left from the older understanding to erode.

The origin stories offer an alternative view, one that does not sunder sex and sexual roles from anatomy nor procreation and child-rearing from sexuality. Certain rare cases of hermaphroditism aside, this traditional view regards gender as a gift, the sexual roles flowing from it as an expression of gratitude for the gift, and the creation of family under the leadership of the father as its natural fruit.

In the choice between the two starkly different views of gender, the stakes are very high. Gender and family together constitute the factory wherein spiritual health is created, and if we lay an improper foundation, everything else in society will eventually go astray—not by next week, certainly, or even next year. But in the generations to come, if our society chooses poorly regarding gender, a high price will surely be paid. The Genesis narrative once again calls us home to sanity. God made them male and female, and in this binary constitution of man the world can find stability and possibilities for true growth and health.

WE HAVE DEFINED *myth* as a truth too big to fit into the small suitcase of mere history, and when we look at some of these abiding lessons offered by the Book of Genesis, we can appreciate just how big those truths are. Our society desperately needs those truths. We need to remember who we are—what is the inestimable worth of the smallest of us, and that we are all brothers, and how precious and worth protecting and honoring is womanhood, and how good it was that God made man to be both male and female.

These truths are vast and are spread over us like the sky. And like the sky, many in our secular culture can look up without seeing them. We need to look up and see the truth that arches over us and that keeps the forces of chaos from raining down upon us, as the ancients thought the sky did. We too easily forget those truths and buy into a false and inauthentic view of human nature. Now is the time to remember who and what we are. Now is the time to read and believe the Book of Genesis.

More Books by Lawrence R. Farley
from Ancient Faith Publishing

The Orthodox Bible Study Companion Series

The Gospel of Matthew: Torah for the Church

The Gospel of Mark: The Suffering Servant

The Gospel of Luke: Good News for the Poor

The Gospel of John: Beholding the Glory

The Acts of the Apostles: Spreading the Word

The Epistle to the Romans: A Gospel for All

First and Second Corinthians: Straight from the Heart

Words of Fire: The Early Epistles of St. Paul to the Thessalonians and the Galatians

The Prison Epistles: Philippians, Ephesians, Colossians, Philemon

Shepherding the Flock: The Pastoral Epistles of St. Paul the Apostle to Timothy and Titus

The Epistle to the Hebrews: High Priest in Heaven

Universal Truth: The Catholic Epistles of James, Peter, Jude, and John

The Apocalypse of St. John: A Revelation of Love and Power

Other Books

Let Us Attend: A Journey through the Orthodox Divine Liturgy

The Christian Old Testament: Looking at the Hebrew Scriptures through Christian Eyes

The Empty Throne: Reflections on the History and Future of the Orthodox Episcopacy

Following Egeria: A Visit to the Holy Land through Time and Space

One Flesh: Salvation through Marriage in the Orthodox Church

Unquenchable Fire: The Traditional Christian Teaching about Hell

A Song in the Furnace: The Message of the Book of Daniel

Ancient Faith Publishing hopes you have enjoyed and benefited from this book. The proceeds from the sales of our books only partially cover the costs of operating our nonprofit ministry—which includes both the work of **Ancient Faith Publishing** and the work of **Ancient Faith Radio**. Your financial support makes it possible to continue this ministry both in print and online. Donations are tax-deductible and can be made at **ancientfaith.com.**

To request a catalog of other publications,
please call us at (800) 967-7377 or (219) 728-2216
or log onto our website: **store.ancientfaith.com**

 **ANCIENT FAITH RADIO**

Bringing you Orthodox Christian music, readings,
prayers, teaching, and podcasts 24 hours a day since 2004
at
ancientfaith.com